FRANCISCO GARCÍA DIEGO

✠   ✠   ✠   ✠

California's Transition Bishop

This likeness of Bishop Francisco García Diego is reproduced from an oil painting in the dining hall of Saint John's Seminary, Camarillo, California.

(*Photo courtesy Chancery Archives*)

FRANCISCO GARCIA DIEGO

California's Transition Bishop

by

FRANCIS J. WEBER

*"His was the blood that faced the guns;
His the quest of the younger sons;
But the wealth he sought is found by few
For the souls of men was the love he knew."*

GEORGE STERLING

DAWSON'S BOOK SHOP
535 North Larchmont Blvd.
Los Angeles 90004
1972

Nihil Obstat:

MAYNARD J. GEIGER O.F.M.
Censor Deputatus

Imprimatur:

✠ TIMOTHY MANNING
Archbishop of Los Angeles

Art work by MARJI DAGGETT

Dedicated
To the Memory of
MARY MEIER
(1878–1970)

*"A woman totally unlike those who
always seem to be pallbearers at the
funeral of the past."*

ILLUSTRATIONS

FOREWORD

THIS succinct, but all-embracing biography of California's first bishop, Fray Francisco García Diego y Moreno, written by the well-known Church historian, the Reverend Francis J. Weber, is based on fresh and recent discoveries. It offers the reader a well-balanced account of a good and worthy man, whose brief episcopate in California was frustrated by governmental interference and local apathy.

The prelate's most successful years were those during which he functioned as a missionary and teacher for the Apostolic College of Our Lady of Guadalupe, Zacatecas, in his native Mexico. He first came to California, in 1833, just a year before the formal secularization of the missions. He returned, in 1841, when Provincial California was crumbling, and died only a few months before the American occupation, in 1846. He lies buried in the sanctuary of Santa Barbara Mission his pro-cathedral, near the rooms he occupied for slightly more than four years in great discomfort.

The two highlights of glory in the bishop's life were his three hour sermon, at Zacatecas, on the occasion of Agustín Iturbide's coronation as emperor of Mexico and his triumphant reception, at Santa Barbara, in 1842, a scene vividly described by Alfred Robinson in his *Life in California*. The centenary of García Diego's consecration, solemnized throughout the state, in 1940, reached its climax in a mammoth liturgical ceremony in the Los Angeles Memorial Coliseum, probably the largest religious gathering ever witnessed in the far west. Other commemorative celebrations were conducted at San Francisco, Sacramento, Fresno, Monterey and San Diego.

Prior to the 1940s, this writer consulted with the late Archbishop John J. Cantwell about the advisability of writing a full-scale life of Fray Francisco García Diego y Moreno. The eminent Los Angeles prelate, while leaving the ultimate decision entirely to my own judgment, felt that California's proto-bishop was not nearly so well known to the general populace nor did he have anything approaching the fame of the earlier Fray Junípero Serra. Fortunately, this writer pursued the archbishop's veiled suggestion.

In more recent times, significant new material has been found in Rome and Mexico concerning the personage of Francisco García Diego, most of which Father Francis J. Weber has deftly incorporated into this biography. Without burdening the reader with the more minute details, the Archivist for the Archdiocese of Los Angeles has succeeded in portraying the complete life of the friar-bishop in a readable, smooth-flowing and concise story. It is here recommended without reservations.

REV. MAYNARD J. GEIGER, O.F.M.

February 1, 1971   MISSION SANTA BARBARA

PROLOGOMENA

THIS particular treatise lends credence to the view that historians, like the more unsavory characters in mystery novels, frequently return to the scene of their initial exploits. It was a quest for details about the life and times of California's first bishop that occasioned this writer's first serious venture into the vast and almost wholly unexplored field of post-mission ecclesiastical activities. The results of that study, published as *A Biographical Sketch of Right Reverend Francisco García Diego y Moreno, O.F.M.*,[1] recounted the trials, frustrations and disappointments of "a good man too long forgotten."[2]

Based largely on secondary sources, the fifty page monograph accounted for about all that was then "known of the Mexican-born Franciscan friar who was consecrated in October, 1840, at the age of fifty-five for the newly erected Diocese of the Two Californias."[3] The principal value of the publication was that of gathering "between two covers the salient facts on the establishment of the hierarchy" in the Golden State.[4]

The considerable amount of documentary evidence unearthed during the intervening decade, from searches of archival centers and visits to such places as Mexico

I

City, Lagos de Moreno, Guadalajara and Zacatecas, amply justifies an up-dated and expanded glance at one of the Pacific Slope's pivotal ecclesial figures.

Interestingly enough, the discovery and assimilation of pertinent biographical data did not contribute, in every instance, to a clearer explanation of the basic facts, as can be illustrated by the complexities surrounding such a seemingly minor point as the place of the prelate's episcopal ordination. Though he had stated, in his first pastoral letter, that his elevation to the bishopric had taken place in Mexico City's "collegiate Church of Holy Mary, Our Mother and Patron, under her title of Our Lady of Guadalupe,"[5] the earliest historical account located the epochal event "in the college church at Zacatecas."[6] Zephyrin Engelhardt added the authority of his approval to the error in *The Franciscans in California*[7] and repeated it, some years later, in an article about Bishop García Diego in *The Catholic Encyclopedia*.[8]

The distinguished episcopal biographer, Francis X. Reuss, compounded the question by having the prelate consecrated "in the chapel of the Franciscan College of 'Our Lady of Guadalupe.' "[9] The first English writer to historically locate the proper surroundings was Father William Hughes, who correctly reported that Fray Francisco García Diego "was consecrated bishop of Upper and Lower California at the famous chapel of Our Lady of Guadalupe, the Mexican national shrine, near the City of Mexico."[10]

That same year, Zephyrin Engelhardt expunged his earlier mis-statements, noting that the Golden State's proto-bishop was, indeed, elevated to the episcopacy in ceremonies "at the famous shrine of Guadalupe, City of

California's initial seminary was inaugurated in the rear apartments off the central corridor of Mission Santa Barbara.

(Photo courtesy Chancery Archives)

Mexico...."[11] That even historians are touchy about their printed indiscretions is evident from one of the friar's footnotes to the effect that the consecration had not occurred "at the College of Guadalupe, Zacatecas, as Reuss has it in his *Biographical Cyclopedia*."[12] The Franciscan chronicler slyly neglected to point out that Reuss most assuredly utilized Engelhardt's own earlier works as his principal sources for the erroneous statement.

The "Zacatecas" myth, long lived as it was, found its way into the first edition of Joseph Bernard Code's *Dictionary of the American Hierarchy*,[13] an error happily deleted in the revised and expanded version issued in 1964.[14] The association with Zacatecas, however, refused to die an honorable death and surfaced again, in 1950, when an otherwise accurate author identified "the Church of Our Lady of Guadalupe, Zacatecas, Mexico,"[15] as the locus for García Diego's investiture with episcopal rank. A partial explanation for such confusion as this about the most basic biographical ingredients of this public man's life can be found in the fact that "when he died in 1846, the whole mission structure collapsed and buried him in its dust."[16]

This treatise endeavors to piece together what extant facts could be gleaned, from a host of sources, into an integral account. Hopefully, subsequent discoveries will further enhance the overall montage of a prelate whose image has yet to emerge with all its salient features.

The author is grateful to a host of friends and benefactors for their encouragement in preparing this study. Special debts of gratitude are due to Fray Rafael Cervantes, Archivist for the Santuario de Guadalupe, Zacatecas; Francisco and Antonia Garcíadiego,[17] the bishop's great grand nephew and niece, Mexico City; Fray Maynard J. Geiger, Archivist of the Santa Barbara Mission Archives and the Reverend José Eucario Lopez, Archivist for the Archdiocese of Guadalajara.

This volume is launched with the sentiments of Leonard Bacon:

Go forth, my book, and take whatever pounding
The heavy fisted destinies prepare.
I know you are not anything astounding,
And, to be quite sincere, I don't much care.
Get off your overcoat, the gong is sounding.
The enemy has arisen from his chair.
He doesn't look so overwhelming, but
His arm is long, Watch for an uppercut.

REV. FRANCIS J. WEBER
June 15, 1971

4

NOTES

[1] (Los Angeles, 1961.)

[2] *The Texas Catholic*, May 6, 1961.

[3] "Notes and Comments," *Catholic Historical Review* XLVII (July, 1961), 262.

[4] Florian Guest, O.F.M., "Book Review," *California Historical Society Quarterly* XLI (March, 1962), 59–60.

[5] Archives of the Archdiocese of Los Angeles, Francisco García Diego, O.F.M., *Pastoral Letter*, October 28, 1840, Mexico City.

[6] John Gilmary Shea, *History of the Catholic Church in the United States*, 1844–1866 (New York, 1892), IV, 351.

[7] (Harbor Springs, 1897), p. 185.

[8] (New York, 1913), IV, 785.

[9] *Biographical Cyclopedia of the Catholic Hierarchy of the United States*, 1784–1898 (Milwaukee, 1898), p. 47.

[10] "Coming Catholic Anniversary," Los Angeles *Times*, October 3, 1915.

[11] *The Missions and Missionaries of California* (San Francisco, 1915), IV, 202.

[12] *Ibid.*, n. 7.

[13] (New York, 1940), p. 126.

[14] (New York, 1964), p. 105.

[15] John Bernard McGloin, S.J., *Eloquent Indian* (Stanford, 1950), p. 3.

[16] Edward T. Haskins, "California's First Bishop," *Catholic Digest* IV (August, 1940), p. 56.

[17] Though the bishop invariably spelled his family name "García Diego", the more generally used form is "Garcíadiego" and it is that version under which the prelate's biographical sketch appears in the *Diccionario Porrua de Historia, Biografia y Geografia de Mexico* (Mexico City, 1964), p. 638.

CALIFORNIA'S
TRANSITION BISHOP

Inasmuch as "there is no significant example in history, before our time, of a society successfully maintaining moral life without the aid of religion,"[1] the careful observer must concern himself about the personages responsible for an area's ecclesiastical growth and development. One such pioneer is Francisco García Diego y Moreno, who is credited with inaugurating the structure of Catholic hierarchial life in California.

Born in 1785,[2] on the Feast of the Stigmata of Saint Francis, barely a year after the earthly demise of his great mendicant confrere and predecessor, Fray Junípero Serra,[3] this humble Franciscan achieved a prominent place in the Golden State's historical annals. Birthplace of this second of Francisco García Diego[4] and Ana Maria Moreno's[5] four sons[6] was the stately Hacienda de la Daga,[7] a few miles from the Mexican village of Lagos,[8] off the roadway to San Luis Potosí. His parents presented the youngster to their parish priest, Father Thómas de Equibel, for the traditional christening ceremonies, at Santa Maria de Lagos,[9] on September 23, 1785.[10]

Just a decade later, Francisco was enrolled at the Seminario Conciliar de San José[11] as a clerical student

7

for the Archdiocese of Guadalajara.[12] In those historic surroundings "his love of learning was stimulated by the example of his three brothers, each rising in his respective state and profession of priest, jurist and physician."[13] During the following six years, he applied himself diligently to the humanities and the arts. As proficient in studies as he was popular among his peers, Francisco cemented friendships there that lasted throughout his lifetime. Two of his closest companions, Anastasio Bustamante and Valentin Gómez Farías, subsequently entered the political sphere where they rose to the presidency of the Mexican Republic. The orderly routine of seminary life appealed to the young priestly aspirant and undoubtedly influenced his decision to enter the Franciscans, upon completing his courses at the preparatory school, shortly after the turn of the century.

Following the customary three month postulancy, at the Apostolic College of Nuestra Señora de Guadalupe, at Zacatecas,[14] Francisco was invested with the religious habit, by Father Ignácio del Rio, on November 26, 1801.[15] He made his solemn profession at the conclusion of the canonical novitiate, on December 21, 1802.[16] The next years he devoted to mastering theology, scripture, liturgy, canon law and ecclesiastical history. The youthful student's intellectual acumen won for him the coveted distinction of *corista predicador,* even before his ordination. He was initiated into the clerical state with the reception of tonsure and the minor orders, in the fall of 1804. Bishop Primo Feliciano Marín de Porras of Linares ordained Francisco García Diego y Moreno at Saltillo's Convent of San Estévan, on November 14, 1808.[17]

From his earliest priestly days, Father García Diego utilized his oratorical talents most effectively. His initial appointment was that of assisting the home-mission program then flourishing, on an annual basis, in many of the established parishes of Central Mexico. The young friar's lingual facility motivated his superiors to ask that he compile a handbook containing the recommended format used in that worthwhile apostolate. The clear, succinct and persuasive *Metodo de Misionar* speaks eloquently of the early years in the priesthood of Francisco García Diego,[18] revealing as it does much about the means employed by the Franciscans in their travels through the countryside enkindling and intensifying the faith of the local populace. Measured by the standards of the time, the *Metodo* was a radical departure from traditional catechetical presentation. Each mission, conducted by a team of friars and lasting from nine to forty days, was placed under the spiritual patronage of Our Lady, Refuge of Sinners. In later years, García Diego issued the *Metodo,* in printed form, as a legacy to the younger friars who had succeeded him, at Zacatecas.[19] By that time, he had carefully revised the text to accommodate the exigencies personally encountered during his many years in the parochial apostolate.

Father García Diego also popularized a novena honoring the Blessed Mother under the title, *Divina Pastora*. Adapted from an earlier format, by Ygnácio Villaseñor, the devotion became widespread enough to necessitate its release, in monograph form, in 1830, by Alexo Infante as *Novena a la Sma. Virgen María en la Advocacíon de la Divina Pastora que se Venera en la Sta. Escuela de la Ciudad de Zacatecas.*[20]

9

On July 4, 1815, Fathers García Diego[21] and Mariano Velasco[22] were delegated to select a site for the proposed Colegio de María Santísima de Zapópan, which had been provided for in a legacy from Manuela Fernández de la Barrena, the Marquesa de Panuco.[23] The location eventually decided upon was some ten miles north west of Guadalajara.

From July 6, 1816, to August 7, 1819, Father García Diego served as Novice Master[24] for the Franciscan community, at Zacatecas,[25] a pivotal position wherein he supervised the spiritual formation of candidates wishing to follow the mendicant life at the Apostolic College of Nuestra Señora de Guadalupe. His daily conferences and instructions[26] set the tone and spirit for a succeeding generation of friars by imparting to others, through word and example, those basic principles upon which his own innermost religious convictions were founded.

With the expiration of his term as Novice Master, Father García Diego was promoted to the lectorate of Philosophy and Arts. His initial lecture, delivered in flawless Latin, on January 4, 1820, was a masterful presentation entwined about the words of Solomon: "Wisdom is better than all the most precious things." He encouraged his listeners to emulate that respect for learning exhibited by such great Franciscan predecessors as Anthony, Bonaventure, Bernardine and John Capistran, men outstanding in their learning and holiness. This they could do, he said, "by drinking at the illustrious fountain from which all wise men have imbibed true wisdom: from the Blessed Virgin Mary, who is the font, the light, the most brilliant star, the full moon, the mistress, the way, the conductress, the channel, the re-

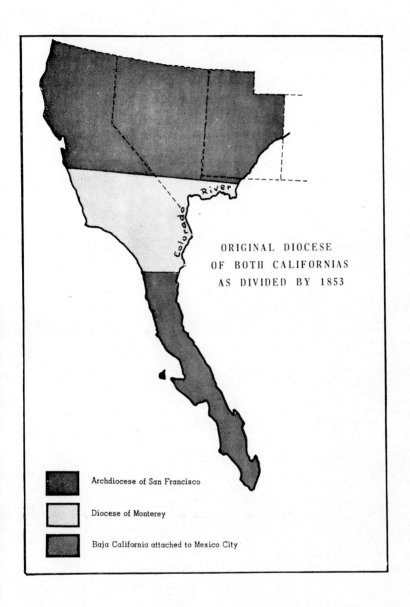

ORIGINAL DIOCESE
OF BOTH CALIFORNIAS
AS DIVIDED BY 1853

Colorado River

Archdiocese of San Francisco

Diocese of Monterey

Baja California attached to Mexico City

Original ecclesiastical jurisdiction.   *(sketch of Anita Weyer)*

Tomb of California's first Bishop

The artistic monument erected to mark the tomb of Bishop Francisco Garcia Diego adorns the wall of the Epistle-side of the sanctuary, in the church of Mission Santa Barbara. The facade is executed in wooden panelling painted to resemble marble, while the capitals of the smooth semi-engaged pillars are carved imitations of Ionic volutes. A pinkish color scheme is broken only by the light blue pediment and the imitation green marble surrounding the medallion.

Directly above the central marker is a circular reproduction of the bishop's coat-of-arms. In the central portion of the episcopal shield is the crowned Madonna and Child, commonly known as the Mater Amabilis. This particular depiction, obviously based on the Refugio of José Alzibar, clearly reflects the Raphaelean influence. A rather crudely-painted border encloses the field with the words: "F. Franciscus Garcia Diego Prim. Epis. Californ."

Atop the seal is the traditional episcopal hat from which descends the six tassels associated with residential bishops. In the apex of the facade is a "precious" mitre and, beneath that, an oversized chalice, symbolizing the priesthood.

The neo-classic influence is obvious in both the sculpture and architecture of the marker. One authority has noted the similiarity of the monument to the entradas and niches designed by Francisco Eduardo Tresquerras. Some have erroneously conjectured that the actual vault extended into the wall. However, in November, 1912, the tomb was located exactly in the corner of the sanctuary, on the Epistle-side of the altar. According to the local chronicle, when the vault was opened, "the coffin was found standing in the middle of the grave leaving about 6 or 8 inches space on either side and more space on the ends; it was found covered with velvet of purple color and having some crosses, and the name of the Rt. Rev. Bishop on the cover being formed of brass or copper nails with large heads. The coffin was found in good, well preserved condition."

(Photo courtesy-Chancery Archives)

The Bibliotheca Montereyensis-Angelorum Dioeceseos, inaugurated by Bishop Francisco Garcia Diego for his seminary at Santa Barbara, in the years after 1842, was reassembled and placed on permanent display at Mission San Fernando. It was formally dedicated as an autonomous collection by Coadjutor Archbishop Timothy Manning, on November 21, 1969.

(Photo courtesy Chancery Archives)

splendent column, *in fine,* all those virtues described by the holy fathers and the universal church."[27]

Though he lived in the relatively sheltered cloister of a religious community, Father García Diego was keenly abreast of the turbulent political current then sweeping New Spain. He had worked closely among the people and understood, from first-hand experience, their economic and social conditions, as well as the pressures exerted on ecclesiastical authorities by an overly protective and paternalistic government. Quite understandably, his natural sympathies inclined towards the land of his birth. An opportunity for publicly expressing those views came, on November 11, 1821, when Father García Diego accepted an invitation to preach at ceremonies commemorating the successful outcome of Mexican independence. His lengthy discourse, as eloquent as it was provocative, portrayed the breach with Spain as the initial step in the reflorescence of the Catholic faith in an era of justice and equality. From that time onwards, the Zacatecan friar was looked upon as an ardent patriot, and his enthusiasm for the Mexican Republic was never seriously diminished, even in the most demeaning circumstances.[28]

The confidence and esteem held for Father García Diego by his confreres is indicated by the host of official positions to which he was elected in subsequent years. He twice served on the college discretory, or board of counselors, and, on July 21, 1828,[29] was designated Commissary Prefect of the missions, a post of considerable importance in which he oversaw and directed the community activities on the frontier, as well as dealings with officials of the territorial government. In 1832, he was named vicar, or vice guardian of the Franciscan community at Zacatecas. Though busily involved with the internal administration of affairs at the Apostolic College of Nuestra Señora de Guadalupe, Father García Diego used every opportunity for continuing his evangelical activities, both in Zacatecas and the adjoining communities.

It was during Father García Diego's tenure as Commissary Prefect that the Apostolic College of Nuestra Señora de Guadalupe received the governmental mandate to involve itself in the missionary apostolate of Alta California, where the friars of San Fernando in Mexico City had labored since 1769. The directive was politically motivated, insofar as the Mexican Republic wanted the Spanish-born priests in those crucial frontier areas, where nationality and loyalty were so closely identified, replaced by a native clergy. Prior to formal Spanish recognition of Mexican independence, in 1836, an exaggerated upsurge of nationalism, manifested itself at many levels of officialdom, including those dealing with ecclesiastical affairs. While pointing out that the Zacatecanos lacked the personnel to assume charge of all twenty-one of California's missionary outposts, Father García Diego dutifully promised to implement the government's request in light of existing Zacatecan commitments.

As part of a long-term program for Alta California, Father García Diego asked fellow friars Mariano Sosa, Francisco Cuculla, Jesus Maria Martínez and Antonio Ánzar to embark upon a fact-finding expedition, early in 1831. The four missionaries left for California and spent the remainder of the year assisting their Spanish-born confreres at San Diego, San Luis Rey, San Juan Capistrano and San Gabriel. In January of 1832, three of the Zacatecanos returned with their recommendations for fulfilling the government's directive that the Apostolic College of Nuestra Señora de Guadalupe involve itself actively in the California enterprise.

After thoroughly investigating the written report and oral reflections submitted by the friars during their California sojourn, Father García Diego recommended that final authorization be given by Franciscan officials for permanently assuming direction of the northernmost Fernandino establishments. Nine of the Guadalupe friars volunteered for the new apostolate and around that small nucleus, the Zacatecan influence was expanded to the last of its many missionary fields.[30]

Viewing "the importance of the subject, there is a remarkable absence of original records respecting the coming of the Zacatecanos and the division of the missions."[31] In any event, by the summer of 1832, Father García Diego and his companions had completed all the necessary preparations and were ready for their journey to California. The government provided the paltry sum of 200 pesos for travelling expenses, an allocation sufficient to defray little more than their transportation to Tepic.[32] During the two months they waited for their ship, the friars busied themselves in preaching and conducting missions and "it was impossible not to feel respect for their character and a degree of veneration mixed with pity on thinking of their destiny and observing their very pious, humble and meek demeanor."[33]

The small band of missionaries finally accumulated funds enough to book passage on the brig *Catalina,* which sailed from San Blas, on August 13, with the newly appointed governor for California, José Figueroa. Already far behind their contemplated schedule, the friars experienced another exasperating delay when a portion of the crew mutinied and left the passengers, including the governor, stranded at Cape San Lúcas. Overly eager to arrive at their destination, the friars rashly determined to proceed northward on foot through the arid peninsula. By the time they had reached Mission San José de Cabo, the missionaries realized the impracticability of their hastily arrived at decision. Father García Diego dispatched a message to the governor, admitting their "utter ignorance" at attempting to continue the "immense journey" through the desolate wasteland. So discouraged was the Comisario-Prefecto that he seriously doubted whether he and his companions would "ever get to the missions."[34]

During the ensuing weeks, the friars administered the sacraments in the sparsely-populated area. Several additional pleas were sent to the governor concerning the "desolate group" of Franciscans and the anxiety about continuance of their work. Ultimately Figueroa regained control of the *Catalina,* and, in early December, departed with the missionaries from La Paz.[35] The last leg of the sea voyage was uneventful, and the Zacatecanos sailed into Monterey, on January 15, to begin a new era in California's ecclesiastical annals.

Soon after his arrival, Father García Diego journeyed to Mission San José to confer with the Fernandino Comisario-Prefecto, Fray Narciso Durán. Though the two friars represented distinct missionary traditions, their common Franciscan heritage fused an amicable relationship that perdured throughout the dozen turbulent years both were spared for the Church's apostolate in California. It was decided that the eight missions northward from San Carlos would be staffed by the Zacatecanos, while the rest of the foundations would remain, at least temporarily, under the spiritual supervision of the Fernandinos. The genial nature of their obviously-delicate discussions was typified by the *concordat-funeral* drawn up, signed and circulated between the two Franciscan communities whereby suffrage obligations were pledged towards friars of either group succumbing at their post. Father García Diego, along with Father José Bernardino Pérez, took up their work at Santa Clara to relieve the aging José Viader, a veteran of forty years on the California scene.

Probably one of the most comprehensive assessments of the local scene was that penned by Father González Rubio who recorded his recollections, in September, 1864, for the Reverend Joachim Adam:

This system, though criticized by some politicians, is the very one that made the Missions so flourishing. The richest in population was that of San Luis Rey; in temporal things, that of San Gabriel. Mine was that of San José, and, although I was promised, as it was on the gentile frontier, it would not be secularized, it, too, succumbed in 1836.

In the inventory made in January, 1837, the result showed that said Mission numbered 1,300 neophytes, a great piece of land, well tilled; the store-houses filled with seeds; two orchards, one with 1,600 fruit trees; two vineyards—one with 6,039 vines, the other with 5,000; tools for husbandry in abundance; shops for carpenters, blacksmiths, shoemakers, and even tanneries, and all the implements for their work.

The fields were covered with live stock: horned cattle, 20,000 head; sheep, 500; horses, 459. For the saddle 600 colts of two years, 1,630 mares, 149 yoke of oxen, 30 mules, 18 jackasses, and 77 hogs.

Twice a year a new dress was given to the neophytes, amounting in the distribution of $6,000. When the Mission was secularized I delivered to the Major-domo then in charge some $20,000 worth of cloth and other articles which the store-house contained.

The church of the Mission of San José was neatly adorned, and well provided with vestments and other religious articles. Thirty musicians served in the choir, and they had a very neat dress for feast days.

Of the Mission of Santa Clara, we can say the same more or less.

The other Missions, called "the Northern," though having been already secularized, were in utter bankruptcy, and the same can be affirmed for the most part of those of the south, down to San Diego; for it was observed that as long as the Missions were in the hands of the missionaries, everything was abundant, but as soon as they passed into the hands of laymen everything went wrong, till eventually complete ruin succeeded, and all was gone. Yet, we cannot say that the ambition of those men was the cause, since, though the Government in the space of four years, divided seven ranches to private individuals—the smallest of a league and a half—yet in spite of this cutting off of part of my Mission lands, the Mission was every day progressing more and more.

We have not to attribute the destruction of these establishments to rapacity; for though we can presume that something was taken, this was not the principal agent of destruction; but the blunder was made in their enterprises and the high fees paid to the Chief Steward and other salaried men, etc.

The Government of Mexico, up to the year 1830, acknowledged a debt in favor of these Missions of over $400,000, without counting other minor debts. Finally, we have to acknowledge that a manifest punishment from God was the cause of the destruction of the Missins, since theft alone could not accomplish it and the subsidy given to the Government would not affect them. On the contrary, left to the priests, the Missions would have prospered, and other establish-

16

ments still more opulent would have been erected in the Tulares, even without any protection from the Government, and deprived of the subsidy of the Pious Fund of $400,000, if the revolution of Spain in the year 1808 and that of Mexico in 1810 had not put an end to the prosperity of the missionaries. If zealous missionaries had been left amongst the savage tribes roaming through this vast territory, from the Sierra Nevada to the Coast Mountains, called then by the priests "Tulares," all would have been converted to Christianity, and would not have perished, as we see them now.

I was able to save only a small relic of these tribes during the pestilence of 1833, in which I collected together some 600 Indians. I would have saved more during the small-pox epidemic of 1839, but my Mission had already been secularized, and I had no resources. I could do nothing for the Indians, who were like boys of one hundred years. It is only with liberality you can draw them towards you: give them plenty to eat and clothes in abundance, and they will soon become your friends, and you can then conduct them to religion, form them to good manners, and teach them civilized habits.

Do you want to know who were the cause of the ruin of these Missions? As I was not only a witness but a victim of the sad events which caused their destruction, I have tried rather to shut my eyes that I might not see the evil, and close my ears to prevent hearing the innumerable wrongs which these establishments had suffered. My poor neophytes did their part, in their own way, to try and diminish my sorrow and anguish.

On my landing in this country, which happened on the 15th of January, 1833, there were in existence from San Diego up to San Francisco Solano 21 Missions, those of San Rafael and Soledad provided everything for divine worship, and the maintenance of the Indians. The care of the neophytes was left to the Missionary, who, not only as Pastor, instructed them in their religion and administered the sacraments to them, but as a householder, provided for them, governed and instructed them in their social life, procuring for them peace and happiness.

17

Every Mission, rather than a town, was a large community, in which the Missionary was President, distributing equally burdens and benefits. No one worked for himself, and the products of the harvest, cattle and industry in which they were employed was guarded, administered and distributed by the Missionary. He was the Procurator and Defender of his neophytes, and, at the same time, their Chief and Justice of Peace, to settle all their quarrels, since the Mission Indians were not subject to the public authorities, except in grievous and criminal cases.[36]

While his duties as prefect did not provide Father García Diego with time enough for all the spiritual ministrations he desired for his people at Santa Clara, the zealous prefect proved to be a worthy and able successor to his Fernandino forebears and one deeply respected and loved by the Indians then residing at the mission. There were no substantial alterations of the buildings at Santa Clara during García Diego's tenure.

The Zacatecanos were not long in discovering that their lines had not fallen in pleasant places. Chroniclers generally agree that they were "as a class by no means equal morally or intellectually to their predecessors."[37] Their inexperience, a certain degree of prejudice by both the neophytes and the Californians, coupled with other problems, caused the friars no little vexation in their new surroundings. "It may be conceded that the newcomers had not the 'drive' of the old missionaries; on the other hand they were facing different and more difficult conditions and from a strict conventual life they had been suddenly thrown into a political, administrative and religious turmoil."[38]

Father García Diego's initial circular to the priests of his jurisdiction reflected a deep concern for the welfare of the Indians. He dwelt extensively on the question of cor-

Bishop Francisco Garcia Diego received his episcopal ordination in Mexico city's National Shrine and Basilica of Our Lady of Guadalupe, on October 4, 1840.

(Photo courtesy Chancery Archives)

Interior view of the Chapel at the Apostolic College of Nuestra Señora de Guadalupe, Zacatecas, Mexico.

poral punishment and using the lash on recalcitrant neophytes. Though deploring the quantity and serious nature of their admitted crimes and offenses, García Diego believed that the lash, as a method of punishment, had outlived whatever usefulness it may have once enjoyed. Not only did the practice run contrary to his own temperament, but the prefect regarded whipping as contrary to the basic principles of pedagogy. He informed his confreres that such punishments had been abrogated, at Santa Clara, and directed that "not another lash of the whip is to be administered to a single neophyte" in the Zacatecan missions.[39]

On another occasion, Father García Diego reminded his priests that "the government had forbidden clergymen to meddle in political affairs, either from the pulpit or in the confessional." Though recognizing that the causes for the directive did not envision local conditions, the prefect advised against "any comments which could be construed, even remotely, as adverse to the government."[40]

Secularization, or the achievement of total local autonomy, always was and is the goal of every missionary endeavor. It was only the extremely slow assimilation of the California natives into the overall civilization program, that accounted for elongating the timetable for Indian maturation in California. The shadows of "forced" secularization were evident, however, in the early 1830s. The movement received an added impetus from the intense nationalism that engulfed Mexico in the years immediately after its independence. While earlier Spanish overtures toward secularization had been generally ignored in California, the concept was an ideal adjunct to the philosophical attitude of the new government and the verbal obsession of its leaders for identifying with individual calls for self-determination.

Governor Figueroa sounded out Father García Diego and his Fernandino counterpart several times about the thorny question of secularization. The Zacatecan Comisario-Prefecto replied that only two of the missions in his district were "viable" and their facilities were needed "to complement the needs of the others." Father García Diego recalled for the governor that the two foundations under question had already been extended to the breaking-point in attempts to meet the needs of the presidios at San Francisco and Monterey.[41] The relatively small populace was an additional reason for García Diego's contention that the whole question of secularization in the California missions should be indefinitely shelved.

Among Father García Diego's most annoying problems were the brazen activities of such men as Guadalupe Vallejo, who repeatedly accosted the missionaries with preposterous demands, most of which were realistically beyond the realm of good sense.[42] It was Vallejo, for example, who accused Father José Mercado of Mission San Rafael with provoking an attack on a band of friendly natives, in the course of which several lives were lost. García Diego, a firm believer in swift justice, suspended Mercado until an investigation could be conducted by two deputized notaries. Fourteen witnesses were interrogated, all of whom agreed that Father Mercado was totally innocent for the "disgraceful deaths occurring in the vicinity of the mission."[43] As soon as he received their verdict, the perfect restored the priest to his San Rafael pastorate.

In the summer of 1833, the Franciscans were asked which of the missions could be secularized in accord with legislation inacted by the Cortés General on September 13, 1813. That law called for substituting secular priests for religious, and handing over all property titles to the natives. Father García Diego answered that, while only San Francisco Solano lacked the ten years specified for autonomy, he felt that it was an inopportune time for implementing the legislation. He pointed out how the enormous distances from the local scene made it impossible for the Congressional delegates to properly understand the character, vices, ignorance, weakness and needs of the peoples in question. Lacking proper supervision, García Diego doubted whether the natives could even continue to exist, much less become useful and productive members of Hispanic society. Reminding the governor that the secularization decrees hadn't been promulgated in the chronologically older missions of the Tarahumaras and Sonora, Father García Diego also wondered how the Diocese of Sonora, already desperately pressed for clerical personnel, could provide priestly ministrations to the widely scattered California populace.[44]

Meanwhile, the restless Mexican Congress, bowing to the proposal of Juan Bandini, passed legislation, on August 17, directing the replacement of the friars by secular priests and the "advancement" of the missions to parochial status. Further elaboration of those provisions came, on November 26, when the government was authorized to adopt whatever measures were necessary to effect secularization of the missions.

Franciscan officials at Zacatecas advised Father García Diego to abide by the measures. With the installation of the diocesan priests prescribed by the legislators, he was instructed to initiate proceedings for transporting the friars to their Apostolic College. Meanwhile, the Comisario-Prefecto pleaded with the governor for patience and understanding in the implementing of new directives.[45]

At a meeting in Santa Barbara, on May 27, 1835, the two Franciscan prefects reviewed their positions and settled upon a uniform response to the gradual, unmistakable encroachment on their missionary prerogatives. In an obvious conciliatory gesture, they offered a counter-proposal to the government consisting of three alternate possibilities, any one of which they regarded as compatible with the Church's overall policy.

Realizing, however, the limitation placed upon the local governor, by the very nature of his office, an accord was reached between the two prefects whereby Father García Diego would personally present the Franciscan dilemma to Mexico City's officialdom. After a visitation to the Zacatecan missions, interrupted for the governor's funeral obsequies at Monterey, Fathers García Diego and Bernardino Pérez departed for the capital, on November 17. By the time of their arrival at Mexico City, "the political complexion of that disturbed land underwent one of its periodic changes. This time it was from right to left, and the new conservative government headed again by Santa Ana, always an opportunist, smoothed the path for the voyaging missionary."[46]

That attitude of the congressional delegates had drifted away from the more unsavory aspects of secularization, at least as far as the California missions were concerned. On June 26, García Diego delivered "a

22

respectful and simple exposition of the problems afflicting the missions" to Joaquín de Iturbide, Minister of Ecclesiastical Affairs. After recalling the historical background of Franciscan endeavors and the benefits that had accrued to the 87,739 neophytes baptized over the years, the prefect, estimated that the 16,864 Indians then under instruction could easily be increased were the clerical personnel available. Unfortunately, he pointed out that only thirteen Fernandino and eight Zacatecan friars remained in California, and many of them were ill and/or advanced in age. In light of the unfavorable prognosis, he suggested, as the "only means of providing priests in Alta California,"[47] the establishment of diocesan form of government. With an imported faculty to staff a local seminary, a bishop could recruit candidates from the native population. Such a "radical proposal," though far from the total answer, offered the only practical alternative to the near-chaos that inevitably would follow in the wake of secularization.

Shortly after submitting his view, Father García Diego was asked to comment on a report received by Ignacio Miguel Martínez about the disturbed political complexion of Alta California. The prefect confirmed that Governor Figueroa's health had long been precarious and that he had died from natural causes, not from poisoning, as some had conjectured. He commented on the various political intrigues following upon the governor's untimely demise, but doubted that there was any organized plot aimed at withdrawing the territory from the national union. The prefect advised the appointment of a governor who would be strong-willed enough to root out the obvious corruption from public office and replace those military men guilty of vice and corruption.[48]

The various proposals put forth by the Zacatecan prefect on behalf of ecclesial affairs in California were discussed in committees throughout most of the summer. Finally, on September 19, 1836, the Mexican Congress adopted, with acting-President José Justo Corro's approval, a six-point resolution calling for a formal study on the feasibility of creating a bishopric for the Californias.[49]

The historical framework surrounding formation of a curial form of government for the Church in the Californias can be traced in 1681, when "spiritual jurisdiction over the Peninsula...was in dispute between Juan Garabito, Bishop of Guadalajara and Fray Bartolomé de Escañuela, Bishop of Durango."[50] The latter, contending that Baja California belonged to Nueva Vizcaya, customarily delegated faculties to California-bound missionaries, until he was rebuked by Rome and told not to meddle in peninsular affairs. The feasibility of advancing the internal provinces of northwestern New Spain to diocesan status was formally suggested, as early as 1760. Renewed impetus for the plan came eight years later with the proposal to form Sonora, Sinaloa and Lower California into a separate ecclesiastical jurisdiction.

In 1775, Bishop Antonio Macaruya informed Father Junípero Serra that the Diocese of Durango exercised authority over future Spanish settlements in California in virtue of the canonical prerogative assigning all undesignated territories to the nearest established jurisdiction. That claim was rejected by Serra, as was the Bishop of Guadalajara's less convincing assertion that

Alta California belonged to his diocese as "a normal extension of the peninsula over which he did have legitimate authority."[51]

On May 7, 1779, acting upon a recommendation from Spanish officials at Madrid, Pope Pius VI created the Diocese of Sonora,[52] comprising the provinces of Sonora, Sinaloa and both Californias. For the first time, Alta California, hitherto a totally independent field of missionary endeavors, fell within defined canonical boundaries. The newly created Diocese of Sonora, entrusted to Fray Antonio de los Reyes, was almost entirely a missionary territory. Communications between Sonora and the Californias by land was impossible and the Franciscan prelate, finding himself isolated from the furthest confines of his jurisdiction, satisfied his episcopal obligations by delegating the Franciscan Presidentes as Vicars Forane for Sonora.

At least one prominent historian feels that "Spain should have asked for a bishop for the Californias, considering the huge territory, even though churches were few and the income nothing."[53] Indeed, the thought of a mitre for Fray Junípero Serra undoubtedly crossed the minds of Spanish officialdom. The Presidente's biographer recalls that after the establishment of Mission San Carlos, "His Reverence learned that a courier at Madrid had written to the Reverend Father Guardian of our college...that a great honor was waiting the Reverend Father Junípero." When word reached Monterey, Serra decided against "the distinction or any other which would forestall his being able to live as an apostolic missionary among the infidels and to shed his blood for their conversion."[54] He took the extreme precaution of

25

writing an influential acquaintance at the royal court, asking that he veto any further consideration of regal favors, should such ever be discussed.

The faculty of administering the Sacrament of Confirmation, bestowed by succeeding Popes on the missionary Presidentes in California, was not renewed, in 1803. That factor greatly disturbed Father Narciso Durán and, in a letter to the Mexican chief of state, written on September 23, 1830, Durán first proposed, for "the spiritual and temporal prosperity of the territory," the erection of the Californias into a diocese and the appointment of a bishop to govern it. The frightful chaos that befell the Church in the post-secularization period strengthened Durán's views that a curial government was about the only effective and practical alternative to the existing status, provided its bishop "does not come to rest, but to work."[55]

The Durán-García Diego proposal was referred to the Archbishopric of Mexico City for further examination. On October 12, 1836, the metropolitan chapter asked Father García Diego to elaborate on certain of his earlier recommendations. The prefect submitted a "minute account of the spiritual inadequacies under which those distant missions presently function and the greater ones which will surely come" unless the suggestion for a diocese is favorably received. As for peninsular California, Father García Diego reported that only five Dominicans were active in the immense territory, extending from the Cape of San Lucas to San Miguel. Lacking spiritual ministration there, the lives of the Indians were hardly distinguishable from those of barbarians or savages. García Diego expressed the conviction that a

Bishop Francisco García Diego consecrated the Church of San Aguascalientes, later designated Cathedral of the Diocese of Zacatecas, on February 22, 1841.

(Photo courtesy Chancery Archives)

The Marian Shrine at San Juan de Lagos was a favorite pilgrimage site for Fray Francisco García Diego during his early years in religious life.

(*Photo courtesy Chancery Archives*)

The Iglesia de Santa María de Lagos, dedicated on May 6, 1741, to Our Lady's Assumption, is still among the nation's most artistic religious shrines.

(Photo courtesy Chancery Archives)

This depiction of *Nuestra Señora Refugio de los Pecadores,*
declared Patroness of Both Californias, by Bishop Francisco
García Diego, on January 4, 1843, was painted on metal,
about 1844, by Eulalio, an Indian neophyte at Mission Santa
Clara.   *(Photo courtesy Chancery Archives)*

government-supported diocesan structure could do much towards alleviating some of the more pressing problems by allowing for erection and maintenance of local educational institutions.

Though there was a more equitable distribution of religious personnel in Alta California, the prefect cited poor communications with the interior of Mexico as a typical and pivotal obstacle to continued reliance on the bishopric of Sonora. The friars, especially those from the Apostolic College of San Fernando, were elderly and many of them in failing health. He noted that the inability to replace them would cause the neophytes, "such tender plants in the faith," to lapse into "the darkness from which they emerged." He recalled that inasmuch as neither the Diocese of Sonora nor any of the apostolic colleges could sustain the California apostolate, the only logical alternative was the appointment of a bishop who could immediately establish a college or house of studies where clerical aspirants from both Californias might be accommodated. Father García Diego felt that the very presence of such a prelate would reverse the downward trend of things "with the sublime dignity and prestige which his office would enjoy among Protestants who would respect him, if not for religious motives, at least as a man who occupies a place of social distinction."[56]

Two days after submitting his observations to the chapter, Father García Diego complained to Joaquín de Iturbide that his confreres in California were "being harassed more now than ever." He asked the minister to intercede with the President of the Republic "to take some drastic measures to alleviate the conditions of the missionaries," reminding Iturbide that if the beleagured friars abandoned their posts, neither he nor his apostolic college would exercise "any further responsibility for the spiritual implications involved."[57]

Shortly thereafter Father García Diego returned to Zacatecas, where he offered a detailed explanation of his interventions to the members of the Apostolic College. Upon the prefect's recommendation, Father González Rubio was named Presidente of the California missions and charged with "seeing, treating and correcting" the Zacatecans remaining at their post.[58]

A series of international problems militated against the immediate implementation of the chapter's recommendations. Poor diplomatic relations with the Papal States, together with the internal turmoil raised by proposals for Texas independence, forestalled action until mid-1839.

Meanwhile, the status of ecclesiastical affairs in California continued its downward thrust. Revolutionary unrest, based largely on personal rivalries, challenged the traditional norms of behavior in the far-away province. The waste and ruin heaped upon the missions during those troubled times provided a sad contrast to the accomplishments of an earlier era.

With the reinstatement in the presidency of Anastasio Bustamante, gestures were made towards solving some of the Church's more pressing problems in California. On June 22, 1839, the metropolitan chapter submitted a terna of episcopal candidates for the envisioned Diocese of Both Californias[59] to the Mexican chief-of-state. After discussing the names with his advisors, the president settled on his former classmate, Fray Francisco García Diego, as the government's preferred choice for the new bishopric.[60] The Archbishop of Guadalajara was then instructed to begin the customary consistorial scrutinium,[61] but a further delay was occasioned by that prelate's extended absence on a visitation tour of his far-flung jurisdiction.

Early the following year, Mexico's ambassador to Rome, T. M. Montoya conveyed the government's wishes to Pope Gregory XVI, along with the name and qualifications of the formally endorsed candidate. On April 6, 1840, Montoya informed Giambattista Cardinal Lambruschini, papal secretary of state, that his nation

considered it absolutely necessary that the Peninsula of the Californias, in ecclesiastical matters, should be governed with entire independence of the Bishop of Sonora to which See it has been until now subject, and that as well as by reason of its vast extent and because of the great distance which separates it from the capital of the diocese, for which reason the Bishop cannot visit it, nor apportion to it all the pastoral aids needed by the faithful, who are very numerous but little civilized.

In order to ensure the effect of such an important resolution, the President, in virtue of a decree of the National Congress, has ordered the drawing up of a complete report from which it resulted that the expediency and utility of the plan was proven by the testimony and opinion not only of the Superior of the Apostolic College of San Fernando, to whose zeal these missions have been entrusted, but also of the administrator of the Diocese of Sonora. A like opinion on the necessity of this measure has been expressed by the former Bishop of the diocese, Don Angel Morales, by the Bishop of the Puebla de Los Angeles, and by the Metropolitan Chapter of the Archdiocese.

In consequence, the legal requisites having been observed, the Government proposes to His Holiness the approbation and erection of this See, and for its first Bishop the Rev. Fr. Francisco García Diego who, to his learning and Christian and political virtues, unites a practical knowledge of that country where he has for some time held the office of Comisario-Prefecto of the missions, as appears from the canonical examination conducted by the Rt. Rev. Bishop of Puebla, commissioned by His Holiness, which report is annexed.

The undersigned may add that the Government desired him to beg His Holiness, in consideration of the vast distance in which this district is, not only from the Apostolic See, but from the Metropolitan See, and because of the necessity in which the new Bishop will find himself in organizing it, inasmuch as one part are neophytes or barbarians, that the said Bishop be granted the extraordinary faculties necessary in order that he may be able to meet all cases and smooth away all obstacles which necessarily present themselves in the organization of the diocese; that he may take along the priests who want to accompany him, be they secular or regular priests, notwithstanding their respective Superiors to the contrary; and that all the missionaries belonging to religious Orders existing there may remain subject to him, excepting only the Comisario-Prefecto and the missionaries who may be occupied in founding new missions and advancing conversions and the propagation of the Faith among the savage tribes; for these missionaries ought to continue using all the faculties granted them by Papal Bulls and Decrees.

It is also expedient to inform Your Eminence that the Mexican Government has made all suitable arrangements that the new Prelate may not lack the proper support necessary in order to cover the expenses and maintain the decorum of episcopal dignity; and that, in addition, according to a decree of Congress, the Pious Fund established for the support of the Missions in California, is to be placed at his disposal.[62]

The various facets touching upon advancing the Church in California to diocesan status were studied by officials of the Vatican Secretariat of State, for several weeks. Also carefully scrutinized was the exhaustive consistorial process circulated by officials of the Guadalajara curia on the worthiness of Francisco García Diego for the episcopal office. On April 27, 1840, Pope Gregory XVI affixed his seal to the papal bulls erecting the Diocese of Both Californias as an autonomous bishopric, independent of the ecclesiastical jurisdiction of Sonora.[63]

The Pontiff's lengthy document recognized that the "great roughness of the roads, the rapid currents of the rivers...and the immense mountain chain inhabited by barbarians" necessitated a bishop, who "powerful in word and deed, might edify the people by his speech and example, correct what is depraved, consolidate what is disrupted, strengthen those who are weak in Faith and enlighten the ignorant."[64] After reviewing the historical background of ecclesial activities in the Californias and outlining juridical succession in the area, the pope minutely spelled out how the bishop's material support would depend on "the real estate which the Mexican Government in accordance with its promise will set apart."[65] A second bull, addressed to the clergy of the diocese, directed the priests to exhibit their new bishop "due obedience and reverence" and to "receive with humility his salutary admonitions and commands."

Meanwhile, Father García Diego, aware of his episcopal candidacy, had resigned as Commissary-Prefect, a post which was filled on July 18, 1839, by Fray Rafael de Jesús Soria. At the same time, officials at Zacatecas entreated Father García Diego to preside at the triennial canonical visitation scheduled for the following July.[66]

Somehow word reached California, early in 1840, that the Holy See was about to provide a bishop for that area. When Father González Rubio, Presidente of the Zacatecan friars, hastily conveyed his congratulations, the bishop-elect acknowledged that Rubio's letter was the first to have reached him from California in three years.[67] As soon as official notification arrived from Rome, Bishop-elect García Diego wrote to the Presidente requesting the priests in the newly created Diocese of Both Californias to offer public prayers of thanksgiving for the pope's concern on their behalf. The clergymen were also asked "to explain the great advantages that will accrue from having their own pastor."[68]

The artistically embellished bulls of appointment reached Father García Diego in mid-summer, along with a governmental directive that he present himself in Mexico City at the earliest opportunity. The bishop-elect took the constitutional oath before President Anastasio Bustamante, on September 19, 1840.

Fittingly enough, the date selected for the episcopal ordination was October 4, the Feast of Saint Francis. The ceremony was scheduled for the National Shrine of Our Lady of Guadalupe, near Mexico City. Principal consecrator was the Right Reverend Antonio María de Jesús Campos,[69] titular Bishop of Rhesiana and the Mitred Abbot of the national shrine. [70]

On October 28, the bishop dispatched his first Pastoral Letter to the faithful of the Diocese of Both Californias. After briefly outlining the reasons for creating the autonomous ecclesiastical jurisdiction, the prelate explained how the government, "prompted by the bond of love which the legislators exercised for those separated by such an enormous distance," had attempted to alleviate the unhappy status of the Church by asking the Holy Father to provide a bishopric for the area. Noting that he had accepted the episcopate "in the wake of our own smallness," he resolved to spend whatever remained of his earthly sojourn at their service, pledging to console them in their sorrows, enlighten them in times of doubt, strengthen them in moments of weakness and teach them the saving message of Christ. Bishop García Diego's optimistic plans for the diocese included primary schools, a seminary and "other pious and useful establishments" geared at blotting out human suffering and furthering Christian morality.[71]

The freshly anointed prelate promptly petitioned the government for payment of the revenues pledged in its proposal to the Holy See, pointing out that California's small population would not be financially viable for many years. He subsequently notified Antonio de Icarza, Director General of the Pious Fund Estates, that he had delegated Pedro Ramírez, a Congressman from Zacatecas, as his agent and attorney for the Pious Fund. A nominal transfer of the holdings took place, on November 2.[72]

A further request was submitted a few days later asking for "special assistance to meet the obstacles and difficulties that seemingly plague my every activity." In addition to a seminary, the bishop sought a qualified faculty "to assist in this great enterprise." He also mentioned the fittingness of erecting a cathedral and episcopal residence. Though he was aware of "the sad condition of the Pious Fund," the prelate was encouraged by the government's pious and paternal determination to leave nothing undone in fulfilling its religious commitments towards the California bishopric. He wanted "competent administrators" to look after the missions as well as special living provisions for the friars. To his request that the Dominicans in Baja California be encouraged to remain at their posts, until adequate replacements were obtainable from other sources, the prelate added a plea for authorization to take whatever priests he could recruit to California. The bishop concluded his memorandum with a plea for additional financial assistance to offset the encumbered status of the Pious Fund.[73] On November 17, Tomás Marín, Minister of the Interior, informed the prelate that the President had concurred and would direct the Governor of California to restore "without any delay or hindrances" the possession and properties formerly administered by the friars.[74]

A number of "business matters relative to the Church in California"[75] delayed the prelate's departure for some months. He made a series of personal appeals to religious communities in Mexico for clerical personnel, but was unsuccessful in obtaining governmental authorization to import Jesuit and Vincentian missionaries from Europe.[76] During his visit to the Apostolic College of Santa Cruz de Querétaro, the bishop ordained Antonio González de Calderán. While in Zacatecas, the bishop consented to consecrate San Diego de Aguascalientes, a church later advanced to cathedral status.[77] The colorful ceremonial, probably the most elaborate liturgical function of his episcopate, was enhanced by the widely-held conviction that the church was among Mexico's most beautiful houses of worship.

Realizing that the governmental pledge of financial sustenance was more promissary than real, Bishop García Diego decided to leave for California with little more than the $6000 which Pedro Ramírez was able to salvage from the debt-ridden Pious Fund. The prelate and his twelve companions, among whom was his niece, Josefita,[78] journeyed to San Blas, where they negotiated for their transportation with Captain Henry John Crouch,[79] on the *Rosalind*. The English brig arrived at San Diego, late on December 10, 1841. Early the next day, the party was enthusiastically welcomed by the local populace and given lodgings in the large two-story residence of Juan Bandini. A week later the bishop administered Confirmation and conferred minor orders on three of his clerical aspirants at the *presidio* chapel.

The bishop's earlier prognosis about the Church's future in California proved to be startlingly accurate. At San Diego and elsewhere, he found the desolation complete, most of the missions in ruins and abandoned, the fertile mission lands and vineyards, with the herds of cattle seized, the Indians reduced to about four thousand and utterly destitute.[80] He also discovered that the good will accorded him by some was not universally shared, especially in certain official circles. Mariano Guadalupe Vallejo, a "peculiarly misplaced Voltairian anticlerical,"[81] for example, felt that "the coming of the bishop is going to cause much trouble," believing as he did that "the age of theocratic domination" was past. While admitting that "new missions among the savages" were desirable, he doubted if anything was "further from the minds of the priests."[82]

The surroundings at San Diego militated against making that town the permanent episcopal seat, though it was formally designated as such by Pope Gregory XVI. Bishop García Diego "concluded, after much thought, that each additional day at San Diego" contributed less to the well-being of religion.[83] The

35

meagre population gave no signs of expanding in the foreseeable future and, at the suggestion of José Antonio Aguirre, a wealthy merchant and ship owner, the bishop decided to relocate at Santa Barbara,[84] the true center of whatever Catholic life yet existed in California. Passage was arranged and, on January 11, 1842, the prelate and his party disembarked at the picturesque Channel City, on the *Guipuzcoana*, where "guns were fired, skyrockets shot off" and the mission bells were rung. The festive arrival of "a functionary that but few in California had ever beheld" was described by Alfred Robinson:

All was bustle; men, women, and children hastening to the beach, banners flying, drums beating, the soldiers marching. The whole population of the place turned out, to pay homage to the first Bishop of California. At eleven o'clock the vessel anchored. He came on shore, and was welcomed by the kneeling multitude. All received his benediction—all kissed the pontifical ring. The troops, and the civil authorities, then escorted him to the house of Don Antonio, where he dined. A carriage had been prepared by His Excellency, which was accompanied by several others, occupied by the President and his friends. The females had formed, with ornamental canes, beautiful arches, through which the procession passed; and as it marched along, the heavy artillery of the "Presidio" continued to thunder forth its noisy welcome. At the time he left the barque she was enveloped in smoke, and the distant report of her guns was heard echoing among the hills in our rear.

At four o'clock, the Bishop was escorted to the Mission, and when a distance from the town, the enthusiastic inhabitants took the horses from his carriage, and dragged it themselves. Halting at a small bower, on the road, he alighted, went into it, and put on his pontifical robes; then resuming his place in the carriage, he continued on, amidst the noise of music and the firing of guns, till he arrived at the church, where he addressed the multitude that followed him.

Santa Barbara was selected to be the "Episcopal See"; and the plans drawn up, for the erection of his palace, a Cathedral, a monastery, and a Theological School. The inhabitants were called upon to unite in forwarding these plans, and the Bishop trusted for resources to the "Fonda Piadosa de California," (Pious Fund of California) in Mexico, for their accomplishment; but as the Mexican Government (Santa Ana) had seen proper to appropriate the fund to less pious purposes, they will undoubtedly remain, for some years, as monuments to the frailty of human speculation.[85]

The "enthusiastic, pious and fervent" greetings were exceedingly encouraging to the bishop. The natives and the *gente de razón* repeatedly entreated him to remain permanently at Santa Barbara. Inasmuch as "the principal portion of the diocese" was centered in the local *presidio,* the bishop eventually did agree to establish his official home at a locale where "security, population and commerce"[86] afforded easy communications, from one extremity of the jurisdiction to the other.

Shortly after taking up residence at Santa Barbara Mission, Bishop García Diego dispatched another pastoral letter to the people of the Diocese of Both Californias. Repeating his earlier-announced plans for the area's future development of Catholic life, the prelate pleaded for assistance in implementing his program for a cathedral, seminary, schools and episcopal residence through establishment of tithing.[87] On May 5, 1842, he appointed José Antonio Aguirre treasurer and overseer of the tithing program in which position he would "deposit the donations, extend my gratitude and grant receipts."[88] This and subsequent attempts at fund raising proved unsuccessful, however, and large piles of stones were heaped up, in several places...as mute reminders of earthly ideals.[89]

A number of minor alterations were made in the living quarters to render the historic mission at Santa Barbara more suitable to the bishop, his students and official family.[90] The prelate's accommodations, along with the overall atmosphere, were described by George Simpson, the General Superintendent of the Hudson Bay Company. He reported that the bishop occupied an ordinary sized apartment, lighted by a small grated window.

This room and its contents presented a contrast which, besides being agreeable in itself, was interesting as an evidence at once of the simplicity of the old fathers, and of the ostentation of their episcopal successor. The walls were whitewashed, and the ceiling consisted of rafters, while articles of furniture that would not have disgraced a nobleman's mansion occupied the floor. The carpet was the work of the Indians of Mexico; the table was covered with crimson velvet, on which lay a pillow of the same material, adorned with gold; and the sofa and chairs had seats of the same costly and showy description. But the gem of the whole was a throne, with three steps in front of it. It was hung with crimson velvet, which was profusely trimmed with tissue of gold; and its back displayed an expensively framed miniature of the reigning pope, painted by a princess, and sent by Gregory to the bishop, along with his diamond ring, as a gift. In this his own chair of state, the good prelate insisted on placing me, though I am afraid that, in thus planting a heretic before his most highly valued memorial of His Holiness, he must have sacrificed in some degree his orthodoxy to his politeness.[91]

The illusory hope for financial assistance from the Pious Fund[92] did not forestall the bishop's recourse to other possible financial sources, though none ever brought about any substantial results. The bishop notified the clergy of the diocese, on January 20, 1843, about his renewed intentions for collecting tithes, asking that the faithful be earnestly exhorted to comply "with the precept of supporting the Church."[93] All Catholics, with the exception of the Indians, were asked to contribute 10% of their earnings as well as a percentage of their yearly increase in flocks and grapevines. Predictably, proceeds from the campaign were pitifully small and the bishop was not optimistic that the future would "promise much more in this meagerly populated area, scattered as it is over such vast deserts."[94] The paucity of Catholics, coupled with their relatively poor economic status, resulted in only about $1,700. The prelate told Governor Manuel Micheltorena that, despite the fact that the churches and priests operated without any funds or support, they would continue serving without stipends. Though he had tolerated a system of stole fees in certain areas of Baja California, the bishop again expressed his personal disfavor at seeing such a plan adopted on a diocesan basis.[95]

Apart from the Pious Fund, the financial position of the Diocese of Both Californias was always acutely precarious. On March 26, 1843, Governor Micheltorena helped to ease conditions slightly by restoring the temporal management of several missions to the Church, on the provision that one-eighth of their annual income would accrue to the government. About a year afterwards, García Diego asked the governor if the quarters used by the friars might be considered sole property of the churches to which they were attached. He also urged that the Church be given dominion over the adjoining orchards and vineyards.[96] When that plea went unanswered, the bishop warned that "the complete collapse of divine worship" was imminent.[97]

Because of the extreme distances involved, Bishop García Diego could not personally visit Peninsular California during his episcopal tenure. To provide for the spiritual care of that vast territory, he conferred upon the Dominican Presidente the title and prerogative of Vicar Forane, whereby all normal canonical problems could be resolved without recourse to the bishop.[98]

On August 23, 1842, the prelate announced plans for a pastoral visitation through the diocese. It was his hope to confer the Sacrament of Confirmation and "personally investigate" the status of Divine Worship, adopting all measures necessary to strengthen and increase the practice of the Faith.[99] The proposed journey was cancelled for "unforeseen circumstances"[100] the following month. Two years later, García Diego was able to resume his envisioned visitation by treks to Monterey, Santa Clara, San Jose and San Francisco. While he may have experienced some happy and consoling incidents on the visitation, as a whole the prelate was depressed by the sight of the once prosperous missions which were then nearly all in a state of poverty and misery.

The initial blessing of the holy oils in California occurred at Santa Barbara during Holy Week, of 1842 and, on June 29, Miguel Gómez[101] became the proto-priest ordained in and for the Diocese of Both Californias. It was also in mid 1842, that the missions of San Miguel and San Luis Obispo were ceded to diocesan administration, becoming thereby the first strictly canonical "parishes" in California.

On October 27, 1843, the bishop requested the Minister of Economic Affairs and Public Instruction to bring the plight of the Church in the Californias to the attention of President Valentín Canalizo. The prelate pointed out that only complete restoration of the Pious Fund could reverse the otherwise-inevitable "extinction of the pueblos" in California. While the bishop expressed a personal willingness to "continue suffering silently," he doubted whether the desperate circumstances of the diocese could be indefinitely hidden from the pope. Nor did he think it likely that the Holy See would name a successor "after my rapidly approaching death" in view of the government's failure to abide by its earlier commitments.[102] Beyond that, Bishop García Diego wondered who "would want to govern a diocese so completely lacking the most basic items and one without any type of subsistence." California's first bishop concluded with his plea for a "minimal respect due the episcopate" with which he had been invested.[103] As for attempts at collecting tithes, García Diego saw "no other alternative to that system practiced in all nations, even non-Catholic ones, namely, that the faithful provide for their clergy directly."[104]

The creation of a bishopric for the Californias necessitated totally restructuring ecclesial life in the area, inasmuch as the superiors of both the Franciscan communities had previously exercised the "ordinary" canonical jurisdiction possessed by apostolic colleges. The obvious need for a careful delineation of their respective prerogatives was demonstrated, in late 1843, when Father Lorenzo Quijas notified the bishop that he had been named Vice Prefect and Vice Commissary for the Zacatecan missions. Bishop García Diego immediately informed college officials that he considered that appointment as "unusual and even injurious" to the religious life of the diocese, pointing out that all ecclesiastical jurisdiction in California originated from episcopal delegation, and not the pontifical charters of the apostolic colleges which had lost their force when the area was advanced to canonical status.[105] Inasmuch as the bishop did not regard Quijas' appointment in the best interest of the diocese,[106] he categorically refused to recognize it.[107]

The perplexed Father Quijas disregarded the prelate's views and began functioning without episcopal approval.[108] When he was confidentially warned by the bishop "with a friendly, polite, tactful and brotherly response" to desist, Quijas answered with a rude letter and then made plans to flee the country, leaving behind orders that the parochial register books were not to be shown to the bishop, a directive that, in itself, aroused a considerable amount of scandal.[109]

In view of the paucity of funds and personnel available, it was a courageous decision, on the part of Bishop Francisco García Diego, to implement his long-expressed wishes to establish a seminary for the diocese of Both Californias. That institution, with all its deficiencies, was probably the prelate's greatest contribution to the Church in California. Shortly after taking up residence at Mission Santa Barbara, 1842, the bishop had inaugurated formal classes for his handful of clerical candidates in the rear apartments off the corridor facing the patio. The embryonic institution functioned for almost two years until the number of students and inadequate facilities necessitated more commodious quarters.

Early in 1844, Bishop García Diego directed Fathers José Jimeno, Juan Moreno and Francisco Sánchez to

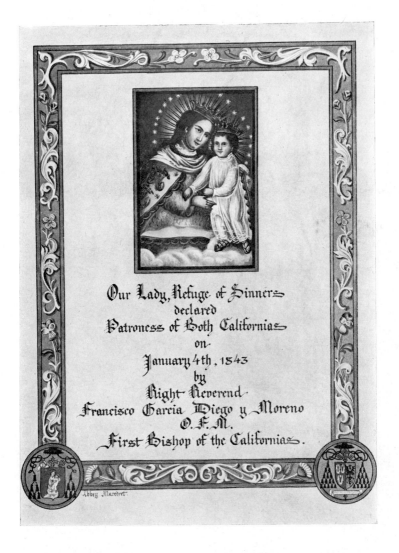

Our Lady, Refuge of Sinners
declared
Patroness of Both Californias
on
January 4th, 1843
by
Right Reverend
Francisco Garcia Diego y Moreno
O.F.M.
First Bishop of the Californias.

*Reproduction of Marian Patronage executed at the Benedictine
monastery of SS. Jean & Scholastique, Maredret, Belgium.
(Photo courtesy Chancery Archives)*

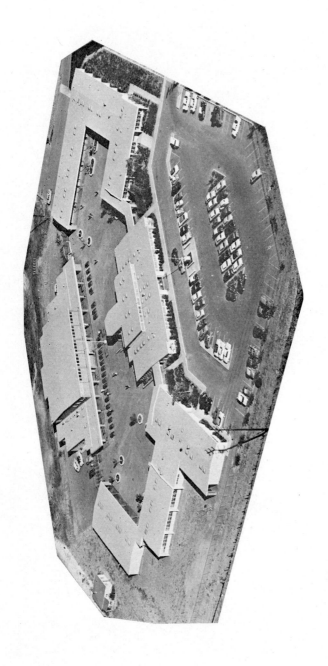

Bishop Garcia Diego High School, at Santa Barbara, California, was dedicated by James Francis Cardinal McIntyre, on March 5, 1961.

(Photo courtesy Chancery Archives)

The tomb of California's initial bishop, Fray Francisco García Diego
y Moreno, was visited by numerous people in 1940, the centennial year
for the erection of the state's hierarchy.

(Photo courtesy Chancery Archives)

CARTA PASTORAL

QUE

El Illmo. y Rmo. Sr.

D. FR. FRANCISCO GARCIA DIEGO,

PRIMER OBISPO

de

CALIFORNIAS,

DIRIGE

A los RR. PP. Misioneros y a sus Diocesanos, antes de su ingreso al Obispado.

MÉGICO.

IMPRENTA DE GALVAN A CARGO DE MARIANO AREVALO.

1840.

petition Governor Manuel Micheltorena for a grant of land adjacent to Mission Santa Ines, on which a permanent building for a conciliar seminary could be erected. The governor responded affirmatively, on March 16, by allotting to the Diocese of Both Californias the four canadas of Sotonocomu, Alisguey, Calabaza and Aquichummo. That original grant, known as the Canada de los Pinos, was augmented, on September 26, by an additional two square leagues on the northern and western sides of the initial area.[110] It was a generous gesture for which the bishop hastened to express his gratitude. The parcel of land, lying on the north bank of the Santa Ines River, which eventually amounted to 35,499 acres, was further enhanced by an annual pledge of $500 which the governor offered to pay personally for youngsters unable to meet the modest tuition.[111]

Construction began shortly thereafter at Santa Ines under the supervision of Father Jimeno. The top floor of the two-story adobe edifice, devoted to dormitory quarters, had a porch or balcony facing the front wing of the mission. On the ground level were classrooms and several apartments for the professors. The handsome structure, with its roof of red tiles, was an altogether imposing and comfortable building ideally suited for the educational needs of the times. The library, subsequently known as the *Bibliotheca Montereyensis-Angelorum Dioeceseos,* already numbering several hundred tomes, was housed in a room near the central part of the old mission.[112] For some unknown reason, "the first educational institution in what is now the State of California"[113] was located, not on the governor's generous land grant, but within the confines of Mission Santa Ines quadrangle itself.

The day of May 4, 1844, was set aside for formally dedicating California's proto-seminary under the titular protection of Our Lady of Guadalupe. Though he had launched the enterprise with practically no financial assistance, the bishop was confident about the institution's eventual success. He envisioned the seminary as "the seed from which zealous and charitable priests will sustain divine worship and, through their teachings and example, maintain the good customs of the country."[114]

Bishop García Diego personally compiled the rules and operational procedures for the seminary. A monastic horarium, much like that followed at the Apostolic College of Nuestra Señora de Guadalupe, at Zacatecas, was adopted. Students were expected to study the traditional theological manuals then used in the seminaries of Mexico, after which they were to present their observations and problems to the faculty for further elucidation.

Unfortunately, the seminary never achieved the lofty goals set by its founder. Even the bishop was forced to say that "in spite of my efforts, little or no success has been realized at the diocesan seminary."[115] And yet, while "only about ten of its graduates became priests,"[116] the institution represented "a transition period between the glorious days of old when saintly and industrious friars reaped a harvest of souls and the modern far-flung province that has passed its Second Spring."[117]

Devotion to Our Lady, Refuge of Sinners, was a hallmark of the Zacatecan friars. In his pastoral letter of January 4, 1843, the bishop announced pleas to place the Diocese of Both Californias "under the patronage and special protection of the most beautiful queen, Mary most holy, Refuge of Sinners"[118] and directed that suitable ceremonies mark the occasion at the various missions. After listening to the traditional panegyric, the faithful were to be exhorted to acknowledge the exalted place of honor and love in the divine economy of salvation occupied by Mary, the Mother of God. The patronage of Our Lady, Refuge of Sinners, has never been repealed.

Unquestionably, the existence of the Pious Fund was "the single most important element in the Holy See's determination to grant jurisdictional autonomy"[119] to the Church in the Californias. When the Mexican Government initially proposed creating a diocese in the northernmost of its provinces, pledges were made that the properties of the trust would be placed at the disposal of that area's bishop and his successors, who would, in turn, manage and utilize the resources along lines indicated by the original donors.[120] That stipulation was plainly stated in T. M. Montoya's petition to Rome:

.... it is proper to inform Your Eminence that the Mexican Government has taken all proper measures so that the new prelate may not lack a decent income which is necessary to sustain the expenses and respect and the dignity of a Bishop; and in addition, according to a decree of Congress, the Pious Fund destined for the support of the missions in the Californias is to be placed at his disposal.[121]

It was in virtue of this pledge that provisions were made, in the subsequent papal bulls, about the new diocese having "as an income for its maintenance in perpetuity the Fund which the same Government promised to surrender."[122]

Early in 1842, Antonio López de Santa Ana, Provisional President of Mexico, asked Pedro Ramírez,

Bishop García Diego's financial agent, for a loan of $40,000 from the already depleted Pious Fund.[123] When Ramírez refused, Santa Ana had that portion of the 1840 legislation bestowing the administration of the fund to the bishop repealed, thereby assuming, on behalf of the national government, control of the trust, an action that was legalized on February 8. His subsequently stated purpose was "to fulfill most faithfully the beneficient and national objects designed by the founders without the slightest diminution of the properties destined to that end."[124] The decree of February 5, 1842 did not impugn, impair or alter the rights of the *cestius que trust,* but rather, obliged government officials to invest and manage the Pious Fund in fulfillment of the wishes placed by the donors.

Further legislation, dated October 24, 1842,[125] directed that the holdings of the Pious Fund with all the deeds, writings and evidences of title thereof be auctioned[126] for a sum equal to their capitalized value at six percent. Proceeds from the sale, as well as the remaining cash belonging to the Fund, was to accrue to the Mexican treasury. It was gratuitously stated that the government would shoulder the obligation of annually paying the missions an amount equal to six percent of the capital value of the trust fund, for the uses and purposes of the trust, as set up by the founders.[127]

In virtue of this latter provision, Juan Rodríguez de San Miguel approached the government, on March 22, 1845, with a request for $16,000, which he claimed was due the bishop and $109,000 the missions and missionaries, from the Pious Fund. He produced evidence that only $603 had been received in the previous three years, with the result that the Church in California was re-reduced to abject poverty. The intervention was effective for, on April 3, 1845, Interim President José Joaquín de Herrera issued an executive order stating that the General Congress wanted the credits and other unsold properties related to the Pious Fund of the Californias immediately returned to the bishop and his successors,[128] in accord with the legislation of September 19, 1836.[129] There are no extant records on which to determine what, if any, property was turned over to the bishop's agent under this decree.

The ultimate financial blow came, on March 18, 1845, when Governor Pío Pico notified the bishop that the missions would be sold to defray the expenses of war with the United States. On the following May 28, the Assembly passed its invalid[130] but effective "Decree for Renting Some and Converting Other Missions into Pueblos."[131]

Though he always harbored a deep-seated opposition to stole fees, the bishop reluctantly agreed to permit the practice where the consent of the faithful could be obtained, "since all remedies, even useless ones, must be prescribed to the fatally sick person."[132] In a lengthy letter to José María Híjar, the bishop pleaded for governmental support to inaugurate a new chain of missions along the coast "to assure the government's possession of that immense territory between San Francisco and Oregon." Such a measure, the bishop conjectured, would give a new vitality to the population, and "provide a boost to agriculture, the arts, commerce, fishing and sailing." He also said that it was imperative for the government to support the Church, through an energetic and equitable system of ecclesial support in tune with local circumstances. Bishop García Diego expressed the probably well-founded view that every other measure, with the exception of restoration of the Pious Fund and inauguration of new missions, "would be merely palliatives and would not remedy the basic problem." In conclusion, he threatened to resign his bishopric and "give the Apostolic See an itemized account of my burdensome situation."[133]

Throughout his episcopate, Bishop García Diego seems to have elicited an ambivalent reaction from his people. Sir George Simpson noted that "all but the better classes were unfriendly to the bishop: the provincial authorities regarded him with an eye of jealousy as a creature and a partisan of the central government; and the mass of the people dreaded any symptom of the revival of a system which had, in their opinion, sacrificed the temporal interests of the colonists to the spiritual welfare of the aborigines."[134]

Several examples of the prelate's image-problems could be cited, chief of which was a carriage accident which occurred on the outskirts of Santa Barbara. According to a priest companion, Father Doroteo Ambrís, "a bull enraged by a crowd of people on foot and on horseback, appeared coming toward the carriage. The crowd continued exciting the bull until it came close to the carriage. Then they gave up their pursuit and celebrated with loud noise and ferocity with which the bull struck the carriage, killing the mule that was pulling it." Ambrís recalled that "the bishop shed abundant tears" on that occasion[135] and, though he apparently suffered bodily injury in the scuffle, the prelate was forced "to return to the mission on foot while men who saw what happened remained."[136] Leandro Martínez, one of the prelate's employees, testified that "no one knew whether the bull was chased outside intentionally or came out accidentally."[137] In any event, "not a single person gave the least aid" to the injured bishop. The event so disturbed Father Narciso Durán that he "felt obliged to give a sermon from the pulpit to the people of Santa Barbara stating that he would be ashamed to have the story of such an incident happening to a bishop of California, allowed to be told outside the locale."[138]

The prelate's health disintegrated noticeably in the early months of 1846. On April 20, he took the precaution of notifying the clergy, that he had appointed two vicars general to govern the diocese, should a vacancy occur, until more permanent provisions could be made by higher ecclesiastical authorities.[139] Bishop García Diego succumbed about midnight, April 30, 1846,[140] probably from tuberculosis, aggravated by acute depression. "Divine Providence," reported Anastasio Carrillo, "has taken from us a grand man, a just soul."[141] The presidio cannon boomed every quarter hour to announce the bishop's earthly departure. Funeral services, to which the entire populace of Santa Barbara was invited, were conducted on May 3. In accordance with the prelate's wishes, he was buried in a specially prepared vault on the epistle side of the sanctuary.[142] On the marker of his tomb was placed the simple, but expressive inscription: *"Hic jacet Illmus. ac Revmus. D.D. Fran. García Diego y Moreno, Primus Epus. hujus Diocesis California. Qui pridie Kalendas Maii, Anno MDCCCXLVI ex hac vita migravit."*

That "the bishop was poor and that his episcopate was but a series of frustrations, no one can deny."[143] Any objective appraisal of Francisco García Diego's relatively short tenure must necessarily touch upon the area's need for episcopal status, in 1840. At least one authority believes that a more advanced type of ecclesial government should have come even earlier, "considering the huge territory, even though churches were few and the income nothing."[144] Generally speaking, however, most commentators regard the creation of the Diocese of Ambas Californias as premature, especially in view of the Mexican Government's consistently obstreputous attitude regarding the only possible means of fiscal support, the Pious Fund.

Sir George Simpson reported that the inhabitants of Santa Barbara initially derived considerable encouragement from the appointment of a bishop, an attitude possibly based on the widely-accepted assumption that García Diego had made some arrangement with the Mexican Government for, at least, the partial restoration of the missions.[145] Few other contemporary writers reflect such optimism, however. Augustias de la Guerra Ord, for example, doubted that the area needed a bishop. In any event, her biographer felt García Diego "was unfitted to overcome the difficulties he faced without priests or money," inasmuch as his only base of popular support was Santa Barbara and "rarely did the discouraged man leave his home."[146] Eugene Duflot de Mofras shared that opinion and predicted, in 1841, that "the influence of the bishop...will not be widespread; his advanced age and his Mexican education will not permit him to take part in any spiritual conquests, nor augment the imposing foundations that are the glory of the Spanish Fathers."[147]

Apparently, the prelate did not enhance his position with the stubborness of his personality. Edward Vischer reported hearing repeatedly about what he called the hypocritical character of the bishop, noting that "his conduct appeared to confirm that description."[148] An equally unimpressed, but openly antagonistic, Mariano Guadalupe Vallejo classified García Diego among those "prelates who suffered from an excess of silly pride."[149] Another even more prejudiced observer recalled that "the bishop rules triumphant, and the wretched priest-ridden dupes would lick the very dirt from off his shoes were he but to will it."[150] Obviously the ill feelings harbored by the *paisanos*, or Californians, for Mexican immigrants explains much of the personal antipathy for García Diego. The bishop himself would, doubtless, have fared better if his cradle had stood in Spain rather than in Mexico.

Francisco García Diego y Moreno gives every indication of having been "a very humble and pious man, unworldly, unselfish and well versed in the ecclesiastical disciplines."[151] While he was not the strong character that the stormy times desparately called for, "it is doubtful if any man could have been a great leader in the troublous times of Bishop [García] Diego's episcopacy."[152] Although chronologically the first Bishop of California, it remained the challenge of his successors to set the scene for a new culture. For his part, the bishop was destined, like his father Saint Francis of Assisi, to taste the stigma of the anticlericalism that pervaded the turbulent, revolutionary Mexico. "He suffered not unto blood, but his natural death was hastened by the unfulfilled promises and greedy chicanery of the men who governed California in the name of 'God and Liberty'."[153]

NOTES

[1] Will and Ariel Durant, *The Problems of History* (New York, 1968), p. 51.

[2] The date of 1765, given by José Bravo Ugarte, *Diócesis y Obispos de la Iglesia Mexicana* (1519–1965), (Mexico, 1965), p. 36, is an obvious error.

[3] A biographical sketch of the prelate, supposedly prepared by the family and verified by ecclesiastical authorities at Guadalajara, appeared in Mexico City's *El Tiemplo*, September 27, 1896.

[4] Francisco, the son of Gaspar García Diego and Rita Gertrudis Mordo, was a native of León, a small village about thirty miles south of Lagos.

[5] The Moreno's were a well-known family. A first cousin of Francisco, Pedro Moreno, was a field marshall in Mexico's War for Independence. His fame accounts for the affixing of the familial name to his birthplace, Lagos de Moreno. Several of Francisco's cousins became priests and at least four were advanced to the bishopric, namely, Juan Cayetano Gómez de Portugal y Solís of Michoacán, José María de Jesús Portugal y Serratos of Aguascalientes, Ignacio Mateo Guerra y Alba of Zacatecas and José María del Refugio Guerra y Alba of Zacatecas.

[6] Mariano became a physician; Salvador a lawyer and José a priest. The family name was perpetuated by Salvador's marriage to Francisca Enriquez de Castilla.

[7] Archives of the Archdiocese of Los Angeles (hereafter referred to as AALA), Carlos Garcíadiego to Joseph T. McGucken, Mexico City, April 24, 1940.

[8] Though its population is now crowding 40,000, Lagos has lost none of that charm and simplicity for which it was known even in the late 1700s.

[9] The parish church, dedicated May 6, 1741, to Our Lady's Assumption, is still one the nation's most beautiful churches.

[10] AALA, *"Certifica: que en el libro número 27 de Bautismos del Archivo de este Curato en el folio 271 frente...,"* August 19, 1966.

[11] The Seminario Conciliar de San José was established at Guadalajara with eight students, December 23, 1696, by Felipe de Galindo y Chávez, O.P. See José María Conejo, *"Sermon en el CCLI Anniversario de la Fundación del Seminario Tridentino de la Arquidiócesis de Guadalajara,"* *Boletín Eclesiástico de Arquidiócesis y de la Baja California* XVIII (October, 1947), 373. For a history of the foundation, see Daniel R. Loweree *El Seminario Conciliar de Guadalajara* (Guadalajara, n.d.).

53

[12] Moisés Vega y Kegel, *Lagos y Sus Hombres* (Mexico, 1952). See also Joaquín Romo de Vivar y Torres, *Guadalajara* (Guadalajara, 1964), p 42.

[13] Joseph J O'Keefe, O.F.M., "Rt. Rev. Francisco García Diego y Moreno, O.S.F., D.D.," *Pacific Coast Catholic Almanac* (San Francisco, 1892), p. 17.

[14] The Apostolic College of Nuestra Señora de Guadalupe, founded in 1707, was, like its sister institutions, an autonomous establishment subject directly to the Commissary General of the Indies. Its chief purpose was "to gather, educate and orientate friars toward a more ascetical life than that common in the provinces." Paramount of its many works was that of "converting the India tribes on the frontier and conducting missions among the faithful in the homeland." See Francis J. Weber, *Readings in California Catholic History* (Los Angeles, 1967), Pp. 85–86.

[15] *Boletín Eclesiástico de Guadalajara y la Baja California* XI (March, 1947). 68.

[16] AALA, Carlos Garcíadiego to Joseph T. McGucken, Mexico City, April 24, 1940.

[17] Several sources give November 13th. In a letter to this writer, the Archbishop of Monterrey explained the discrepancy *"por las guerras intestinas que ha padecido México...."* See AALA, Alfonso Espino to Francis J. Weber, Monterrey, December 5, 1966.

[18] Maynard J. Geiger, O.F.M. (Trans.), "El Método de Misionar," *Provincial Annals* VI (October, 1944), 14.

[19] No copy of that initial edition, printed at Zacatecas, March 11, 1841, his been seen by this writer. The text was incorporated into José Francisco Sotomayor's *Historia del Apostólico Colegio de Nuestra Señora de Guadalupe de Zacatecas* (Zacatecas, 1874), pp. 237–255. A more modern, but less well-edited text was released, in 1931, by Archbishop Francisco Orozco y Jimenez, as *Método de Misionar Entre Fieles, que ha Usado Siempre el Colegio Apostólico de Ntra. Sra. de Guadalupe de Zacatecas*. That fourteen page monograph was published at Guadalajara by Talleres Graficos "Radio " It also appeared in the *Boletín Eclesiástico de la Arquidiócesis de Guadalajara y de la Baja California* III (January, 1932), 10–20. The *Método* was translated into English by Maynard J. Geiger, O.F.M., and appeared in *Provincial Annals* VI (October, 1944), 14–26.

[20] AALA, Copy from one in the possession of Harry Downie.

[21] Juan Cruz Rúiz de Cabañas, *Historia Breve y Compendiosa del Colegio Apostólico de Propaganda Fide de Ntra. Sra. de Zapopan* (Guadalajara, 1925), p. 14.

[22] Alfonso de Alba Martin, *Entonces y Ahora* (Guadalajara, 1944), p. 97.

[23] See the 1931 edition of *Método de Misionar,* p. 1., Prologue by Francisco Orozco y Jimenez.

[24] Peter T. Conmy, "Francisco García Diego y Moreno, First Catholic Bishop of California," *The Grizzly Bear* LXVI (February, 1940), 3.

[25] AALA, Pascuál Rúiz, O.F.M., "Datos et Documentos" III.

[26] In the Santa Barbara Mission Archives is a 193 page manuscript of sermons, written in a neat, almost print-like writing entitled "Apuntes utiles para hacer sermones para Misión y algunos panegíricos, Año de 1823."

[27] AALA, Discourse Given to the Clerics at the Beginning of Their Course of Philosophy," January 4, 1820. (Transcript). Another translation can be found in the *Provincial Annals* X (July, 1947), 82–85, by Maynard J. Geiger, O.F.M.

[28] AALA, Sermon que en el Solemnisima Función que hizo este Colegio de N.S. de Guadalupe de Zacatecas.... (Guadalajara, 1822). Imprenta de D. Mariano Rodríguez, 32pp. He noted for example, how later "political convulsions have torn my heart apart for they have ruptured the peace and tranquility that I seek for my flock." See AALA, Francisco García Diego, O.F.M. to José Maria Híjar, n.p., June 17, 1845.

[29] Maynard J. Geiger, O.F.M., *Franciscan Missionaries in Hispanic California*, 1769–1848. *A Biographical Dictionary* (San Marino, 1969), p. 98.

[30] The Zacatecans had previously toiled in the missionary fields of Texas. See Michael B. McCloskey, O.F.M., *The Formative Years of the Missionary College of Santa Cruz of Querétaro*, 1683–1733 (Washington, 1955).

[31] Hubert Howe Bancroft, *History of California* (San Francisco, 1886), III, 319.

[32] AALA, Francisco García Diego, O.F.M. to José Figueroa, San José del Cabo, September 5, 1832.

[33] Quoted in Francis J. Weber, *A Biographical Sketch of Right Reverend Francisco García Diego y Moreno, O.F.M.* (Los Angeles, 1961), p. 6.

[34] AALA, Francisco García Diego, O.F.M. to José Figueroa, San José del Cabo, September 5, 1832.

[35] AALA, Francisco García Diego, O.F.M., to José Figueroa, Casitas, October 6, 1832.

[36] Abridged from Patrick Joseph Thomas, *Our Centennial Memoir. Founding of the Missions* (San Francisco, 1877), Pp. 41–45.

[37] Hubert Howe Bancroft, *op. cit.*, III, 321.

[38] Albert R. Bandini, "A Bishop Comes to California," *American Ecclesiastical Review* CIII (September, 1940), 255.

[39] AALA, Francisco García Diego, O.F.M. to friars, Santa Clara, July 4, 1833.

[40] AALA, Francisco García Diego, O.F.M. to friars, n.p., June 20, 1834.

[41] AALA, Francisco García Diego, O.F.M. to José Figueroa, Santa Clara, April 15, 1833.

[42] AALA, Francisco García Diego, O.F.M. to José Figueroa, Santa Clara, June 15, 1833.

[43] AALA, Francisco García Diego, O.F.M. to José Figueroa, Santa Clara, June 19, 1834.

[44] AALA, Francisco García Diego to José Figueroa, Santa Clara, October 15, 1833.

[45] AALA, Francisco García Diego, O.F.M. to José Figueroa, Santa Clara, August 3, 1835.

[46] Herbert Ingram Priestly, *The Mexican Nation* (New York, 1930), p. 217.

[47] AALA, Francisco García Diego, O.F.M., to Joaquín de Iturbide, Mexico City, June 27, 1836.

[48] AALA, Francisco García Diego, O.F.M. to Mexican Government, Mexico City, July 20, 1836.

[49] AALA, Secretaria de Justicia y Negocios Eclesiásticos-decree, Mexico City, September 19, 1836. A translation of this document appears in Francis J. Weber, *Documents of California Catholic History* (Los Angeles, 1965), Pp. 43–44.

⁵⁰ Francis J. Weber, "The Development of Ecclesiastical Jurisdiction in the California," *Records of the American Catholic Historical Society* LXXV (June, 1964), 98.

⁵¹ Francis J. Weber, "Church Authority is Traced," *The Tidings*, March 17, 1967.

⁵² See Edwin A. Ryan, "Ecclesiastical Jurisdiction in the Spanish Colonies," *Catholic Historical Review* V (April, 1919), 15-18.

⁵³ Maynard J. Geiger, O.F.M., *The Life and Times of Fray Junípero Serra* (Washington, 1959), II, 344.

⁵⁴ Francis J. Weber, "Fr. Serra Avoided Honor Of Being Named Bishop," *The Tidings*, August 22, 1969.

⁵⁵ Zephyrin Engelhardt, O.F.M., *The Missions and Missionaries of California* (San Francisco, 1913), III, 494.

⁵⁶ AALA, Francisco García Diego, O.F.M. to Metropolitan Chapter, Mexico City, October 15, 1836.

⁵⁷ AALA, Francisco García Diego, O.F.M. to Joaquín de Iturbide, Mexico City, October 17, 1836.

⁵⁸ AALA, Francisco García Diego, O.F.M. to González Rubio, O.F.M., Zacatecas, June 19, and July 27, 1837.

⁵⁹ AALA, Francisco García Diego, O.F.M., *Pastoral Letter*, Mexico City, October 28, 1840.

⁶⁰ AALA, The chapter's terna carried the names of Francisco García Diego, O.F.M., José María Guzmán, O.F.M. and Joaquín Soriano, C.P.M.

⁶¹ See AALA for a copy of the eighty-eight page *Consistorial Process* obtained from the Secret Vatican Archives through the courtesy of the Reverend John B. McGloin, S.J.

⁶² See Jackson Ralston, *Appendix II. Foreign Relations of the United States*, 1902. *United States vs. Mexico. In the Matter of the Case of the Pious Fund of the Californias* (Washington, 1903), Pp. 436-437 for an alternate translation.

⁶³ Boundaries for the vast new diocese were: the Colorado River in the east; the 42° degree of north latitude (Oregon line); the Pacific Ocean in the west and all of Baja California.

⁶⁴ AALA, Gregory XVI to Francisco García Diego, O.F.M., Rome, April 27, 1840. See also Jesús García Gutiérrez (comp.), *Bulario de la Iglesia Mejicana* (Mexico, 1951), Pp. 66-69.

⁶⁵ AALA, Gregory XVI to Faithful of the Diocese of Both Californias, Rome, April 27, 1840.

⁶⁶ AALA, Francisco García Diego, O.F.M. to Plutarco García Diego, Lagos de Moreno, July 4, 1839.

⁶⁷ AALA, Francisco García Diego, O.F.M. to González Rubio, O.F.M., Zacatecas, February 1, 1840.

⁶⁸ AALA, Francisco García Diego, O.F.M. to González Rubio, Zacatecas, August 11, 1840.

⁶⁹ Not José María de Jesús Belaunzarán as stated by Emeterio Valverde Telles, *Bio-Bibliográfica Eclesiástica Mexicana (1821-1943)* (Mexico, 1949), 1, 320.

⁷⁰ Francisco Luján, *El Colegio de Guadalupe, O Bosquejo Cronológico Histórico y Biografía del Colegio Apostólico de Maria Santisima de Guadalupe de Zacatecas* III (1889), 120-124.

[71] AALA, Francisco García Diego, O.F.M., *Pastoral Letter*, Mexico City, October 28, 1840.

[72] AALA, Francisco García Diego, O.F.M. to Antonio de Icarza, Mexico City, October 30, 1840.

[73] AALA, Francisco García Diego, O.F.M. to Government, Mexico City, November 7, 1840.

[74] Tómas Marín to Francisco García Diego, O.F.M., Mexico City, November 17, 1840. Quoted in Jackson Ralston, *op. cit.*

[75] AALA, Francisco García Diego, O.F.M. to Departmental Assembly, Mexico City, November 30, 1840.

[76] AALA, Francisco García Diego, O.F.M. to Minister of Interior, n.p., July 16, 1841. What sentiments there may have been for allowing the Jesuits to return quickly evaporated with the restoration of the Santa Ana regime. See Patrick Joseph Foote, S.J., *Some Historical Notes of Men and Events That Led Up to the Return of the Jesuits to California* (San Francisco, n.d.), Pp. 4–5.

[77] The artistic church and its richly carved portico, formerly known under the patronage of Nuestra Señora de la Ascensión, was begun, in 1622, and dedicated, in 1752. The facade of the strict neo-classical building, is filled with life-size statues of Christ and the apostles. An inscription on both sides of the external walls reads: "*Esta santa Iglesia parroquial se conságro el día 22 de Febrero de 1841 por el Ylmo. y Rmo. Sr. D. Fr. Fran. García Diego, primer Obispo de Californias. A.M.D.G.*"

[78] For some biographical information on the prelate's niece, see Thomas F. Prendergast, *Forgotten Pioneers. Irish Leaders in Early California* (San Francisco 1942), p. 43. Also in the bishop's company were Fathers Francisco Sánchez and Miguel Muro from Zacatecas; six seminarians: Subdeacon José Miguel Gómez; Antonio Jiménez, José María Rosales and Doroteo Ambrís and two younger boys, Alejo Salmón and Leandro Martínez; and an elderly companion for the prelate's niece.

[79] See William Hughes, "Coming Catholic Anniversary," Los Angeles *Times*, October 3, 1915.

[80] John Gilmary Shea, *The Hierarchy of the Catholic Church in the United States* (New York 1886), p. 170.

[81] Albert R. Bandini, *op. cit.*, 263.

[82] Quoted in Gerald J. Geary, *The Secularization of the California Missions* (1810–1846) (Washington, 1934), p. 180.

[83] AALA, Francisco García Diego, O.F.M. to Juan Alvarado, Santa Barbara, April 25, 1842.

[84] Maynard J. Geiger. O.F.M., *Mission Santa Barbara* 1782–1965 (Santa Barbara, 1965), p. 120.

[85] From *Life in California*, reproduced in *Noticias* VI (Summer, 1960), 4–5.

[86] AALA, Francisco García Diego, O.F.M. to Juan Alvarado, Santa Barbara, April 25, 1842.

[87] AALA, Francisco García Diego, O.F.M., *Pastoral Letter*, Santa Barbara, February 4, 1842.

[88] AALA, Francisco García Diego, O.F.M. to Antonio Aguírre, Santa Barbara, May 5, 1842.

[89] Alfred Robinson, *Life in California* (Oakland, 1947), p. 124.

[90] AALA, Francisco García Diego, O.F.M. to Juan Alvarado, Santa Barbara, May 6, 1842.

[91] Quoted in Maynard J. Geiger, O.F.M., *Mission Santa Barbara*, Pp. 122–123.

[92] See Francis J. Weber, "The United States Versus Mexico: The Final Settlement of the Pious Fund of the Californias," *Southern California Quarterly* LI (June, 1969), 97–152.

[93] AALA, Francisco García Diego, O.F.M. to Priests, Santa Barbara, January 20, 1843.

[94] AALA, Francisco García Diego O.F.M. to Lucas Alamón, Santa Barbara, September 12, 1843.

[95] AALA, Francisco García Diego, O.F.M. to Minister of Exterior Relations, Santa Barbara, September 9, 1843.

[96] AALA, Francisco García Diego, O.F.M. to Manuel Micheltorena, Santa Barbara, June 8, 1844.

[97] AALA, Francisco García Diego, O.F.M. to Manuel Micheltorena, n.p., September 5, 1844.

[98] AALA, Francisco García Diego, O.F.M., to Ignacio Ramírez de Arrellano, O.P., Santa Barbara, December 4, 1842 and Francisco García Diego, O.F.M. to Gabriel González, O.P., Santa Barbara, August 16, 1843.

[99] AALA, Francisco García Diego, O.F.M. to Zacatecan friars, Santa Barbara, August 23, 1842.

[100] AALA, Francisco García Diego, O.F.M. to Zacatecan friars, Santa Inés, September 10, 1842.

[101] Miguel Gómez subsequently returned to his native Mexico where he succumbed in 1856.

[102] For a sketch of the four year inter-regnum that actually occurred after the prelates death, see Francis J. Weber, *Catholic Footprints in California* (Newhall, 1970), Pp. 199–200.

[103] AALA, Francisco García Diego, O.F.M. to Minister of Economic Affairs and Public Instruction, Santa Barbara, October 27, 1843.

[104] AALA, Francisco García Diego, O.F.M. to Manuel Micheltorena, n.p., September 6, 1844.

[105] AALA, Francisco García Diego, O.F.M. to Guardian, Santa Barbara, December 15, 1843.

[106] AALA, Francisco García Diego, O.F.M. to José Lorenzo Quijas, Santa Barbara, December 15, 1843.

[107] AALA, Francisco García Diego, O.F.M. to Lorenzo Quijas, O.F.M., Santa Barbara, December 19, 1843.

[108] For details about an earlier altercation by the seemingly conscientous Quijas, see George Tays, "Mariano Guadalupe Vallejo and Sonoma," *California Historical Society Quarterly* XVI (September, 1937), 240ff.

[109] AALA, Francisco García Diego, O.F.M. to Guardian, Santa Barbara, May 26, 1844.

[110] Alpheus Felch, *Lands of the Catholic Church. Opinion of the Board Confirming the Claim* (San Francisco, 1855), p. 2.

[111] AALA, Francisco García Diego, O.F.M. to Manuel Micheltorena, Santa Barbara, February 27, 1844.

[112] Francis J. Weber, *A Bibliophilic Odyssey* (Los Angeles, 1969), p. 13.

[113] Kurt Baer, *The Treasures of Mission Santa Ines* (Fresno, 1956), p. 93. This building is not to be confused with that later erected for the college some distance away, at San Isidro, which functioned until 1882.

[114] AALA, Francisco García Diego, O.F.M. to Manuel Micheltorena, Santa Barbara, May 4, 1844.

[115] AALA, Francisco García Diego, O.F.M. to José María Híjar, n.p., August 8, 1845.

[116] Finbar Kenneally, O.F.M., *The Catholic Seminaries of California As Educational Institutions, 1840–1850* (Toronto, 1956), p. 6. The first students to complete their sacerdotal training at Santa Inés, Fathers Prudencio Santillan, José de los Santos and Doroteo Ambrís were ordained, on January 1, 1846.

[117] Zephyrin Engelhardt, O.F.M., quoted in Francis J. Weber, *A Guide to Saint John's Seminary* (Los Angeles, 1966), p. 6.

[118] AALA, Francisco García Diego, O.F.M., *Pastoral Letter*, Santa Clara, January 4, 1843. Named as secondary patrons were Saints Francis of Assisi and Francis de Sales.

[119] Francis J. Weber, *The United States Versus Mexico: The Final Settlement of the Pious Fund* (Los Angeles, 1969), Pp. 54–55.

[120] *Laws of Mexico Relating to the Pious Fund* (The Hague, 1902), p. 7.

[121] *Letter of the Mexican Legation at Rome to the Holy See, Dated April 6, 1840, and Affidavit of the Most Reverend Patrick William Riordan. The Case of the Pious Fund of the Californias* (n.p., n.d.), p. 3.

[122] Francis J. Weber, *A Biographical Sketch of Right Reverend Francisco García Diego y Moreno, O.F.M.*, p. 20.

[123] Juan Rodríguez de San Miguel, *Documentos Relativos Al Piadoso Fondo de Misiones para Conversión y Civilización de las Numerosas Tribus Barbaras de la Antigua y Nueva California* (Mexico, 1845), p. 8.

[124] "Decreto por el que reasumió el gobierno lo administración e inversión del fondo piadoso de Californias," *Extracts from Works Referred to in the "Brief History of the Pious Fund of California" Annexed to the Memorial, and in the Argument of Claimant's Counsel* (San Francisco, 1872), Pp. 66–67.

[125] For the text of the decree, see Thaddeus Amat, C.M. and Joseph Sadoc Alemany, O.P., *Comisión Mixta Reclamaciones de Mexico y Los Estados-Unidos* (Mexico, 1876), Pp. 258–261.

[126] The exact sale price was estimated by Juan Rodríguez de San Miguel to be $600,000 plus $1,075,182.25 owed by the government.

[127] Andrew F. Burke, "The Pious Fund," *Academy Scrapbook* V (1959), 91.

[128]*Laws of Mexico,* Pp. 9–10.

[129]See Note 123, *ante.*

[130]The sales resulting from this legislation were subsequently declared invalid by the United States government.

[131]A brief from acting President José Joaquín Herrera suspending the sale, issued on November 4, 1845, was never honored in California.

[132]AALA, Francisco García Diego, O.F.M. to Pío Pico, Santa Barbara, July 4, 1845.

[133]AALA, Francisco García Diego, O.F.M. to José María Híjar, n.p., August 8, 1845.

[134]*Narrative of a Journey Round the World* (London, 1847), I, 388.

[135]*Scritture Originali Referite Nelle Congregazione Generali.* I Parte. 1860. Vol. 985. Pp. 16–166.

[136]Thaddeus Amat, C.M., *Scritture. . . .,* Pp. 405–414.

[137]Quoted in Maynard J. Geiger, O.F.M., *Mission Santa Barbara,* p. 129.

[138]*Scritture. . . .,* Pp. 209–212.

[139]AALA, Francisco García Diego, O.F.M. to Clergy of the Diocese of Both Californias, Santa Barbara, April 20, 1846

[140]Kurt Baer, *Painting and Sculpture at Mission Santa Barbara* (Washington, 1955) p. 72.

[141]Quoted in Zephyrin Engelhardt, O.F.M., *Santa Barbara Mission* (San Francisco, 1923), p. 259.

[142]See Francis J. Weber, "Monument to Bishop A Paradox," *The Tidings,* March 8, 1968. The prelate's tomb was subsequently opened, several decades later."The grave was found located exactly in the corner of the sanctuary on the epistle side of the altar, and being walled up with brick and stone on both sides and ends and being covered with red-wood planks over which earth and gravel was spread about a foot in thickness. The coffin was found standing in the middle of the grave leaving about 6 or 8 inches space on each side and more space on the ends; it was found covered with velvet of purple color and having some crosses, and the name of the Rt. Rev. Bishop on the cover being formed of brass or copper nails with large heads. The coffin was found in good, well preserved condition—It was not opened—the walls of the grave were built higher of brick so as to reach the new concrete floor a projection being left on the walls, wherever to put stone or marble slabs to cover the grave." *Cronica Franciscana Conventus FF. Minorum S.P.N. Francisco Ad. S. Barbarum.* Vol I, Pp. 210–211.

[143]Maynard J. Geiger, O.F.M., *Mission Santa Barbara,* p. 131.

[144]Maynard J. Geiger, O.F.M., *The Life and Times of Fray Junípero Serra,* II, 344.

[145]*Op. cit.,* I, 338.

[146]Francis Price and William H. Ellison (Trans.), *Occurrences in Hispanic California* (Washington, 1956), p. 87.

[147]Marguerite Eyer Wilbur (Trans.), *Duflot de Mofras' Travels on the Pacific Coast* (Santa Ana, 1937), I, 140.

[148]Quoted in Erwin Gustav Gudde, "Edward Vischer's First Visit to California," *California Historical Society Quarterly* XIX (September, 1940), 201.

[149]Quoted by John B. McGloin, S.J., *California's First Archbishop* (New York, 1966), p. 362.

[150]John C. Jones as quoted in William E. North, *Catholic Education in Southern California* (Washington, 1936), p. 79.

[151]Albert R. Bandini, *op. cit.*, 266.

[152]Edward T. Haskins, "California's First Bishop," *Catholic Digest* IV (August, 1940), 61.

[153]Arthur D. Spearman, S.J., *Our Lady Patroness of the Californias* (Santa Clara, 1966), p. 3.

APPENDIX

Clergy in the Diocese of Both Californias—1846

Doroteo Ambrís	d.1883	Secular	Mexico	Monterey
José Antonio Anzar	c.1793-1874	Franciscan	Mexico	San Juan Bautista
Narciso Durán	1776-1846	Franciscan	Spain	Santa Barbara
Tomás Eleuterio Esténaga	1790-1847	Franciscan	Spain	San Gabriel
Miguel Gómez	d.1856	Secular	Mexico	San Luis Obispo
Gabriel González	1801-1868	Dominican	Spain	San Jose del Cabo-BC
José María de Jesús González Rubio	1804-1875	Franciscan	Mexico	Santa Barbara
Antonio Jimenez del Recio	d.1853	Secular	Mexico	Los Angeles
Antonio Jimeno	d.1876	Franciscan	Mexico	Santa Barbara
José Joaquín Jimeno	1804-1856	Franciscan	Mexico	Santa Inés
Tomás Mansilla		Dominican		Santo Tomas-BC
Vicente Oliva	1780-1848	Franciscan	Spain	San Diego
Blaz Ordaz	1792-1850	Franciscan	Spain	San Fernando
Ignacio Ramírez de Arrellano		Dominican		San Antonio-BC
José María Rosales		Secular	Mexico	San Buenaventura
Francisco Sánchez	1813-1884	Franciscan	Mexico	Santa Inés
Prudencio Santillán		Secular	Mexico	San Francisco
Vicente Sotomayor		Mercedarian		Comondu-BC
José María del Refugio Suarez del Reál	c.1804-18-?	Franciscan	Mexico	Santa Clara
José María Zalvidea	1780-1846	Franciscan	Spain	San Gabriel

DATE DUE